THE LITTLE BOOK OF
DANGEROUS ANIMALS

Written by Louise Malo

THE LITTLE BOOK OF
DANGEROUS
ANIMALS

This edition first published in the UK in 2008
By Green Umbrella Publishing

© Green Umbrella Publishing 2008

Publishers Jules Gammond and Vanessa Gardner

Printed and bound in China

ISBN 978-1-905828-13-5

Contents

Chapter 1

Introduction

ALL ANIMALS DESERVE TO BE TREated with respect. But, some animals gain respect more quickly than others, just by their sheer size, body weight, the teeth or jaws they have or for the deadly sting or bite they might give. Dangerous animals are feared by man the world over but it is usually the local population – despite their knowledge and understanding of such creatures – who will usually come in for attack quite simply because they live and work in such close proximity. It would be easy for humans to become complacent, given their dominance on Earth, however, beware. Just by the very nature of survival and what that means to the animals, some see man as a threat – or worse – their next meal. Perhaps it would be prudent to bear in mind though, that encountering a dangerous animal may be a terrifying experience,

but it is probably man who is by far the most dangerous animal of them all.

What is remarkable about animal groups is that they are related to one another, extremely distantly in many cases, but all have descended from common ancestors. During the millions of years that animals have lived on the Earth, gradual changes have taken place so that new species have evolved and formed. Interestingly, of the million and a half species that live today, these only represent about one per cent of all the animal species that have ever roamed the planet. The vast majority became extinct in ages past, leaving their fossils as a record allowing the path of evolution to be explored.

All species are limited by geographical boundaries and each needs a habitat in which to live. The tundra, adjacent to the polar regions, with its low-growing vegetation and limited number of species, is by its very nature unstable, while the waters around the Antarctic ice cap are rich in food. Tropical rainforests stretch from Florida to Brazil, across Africa, India and southeast Asia to Queensland in Australia. The existence of these forests is dependent on how much moisture they can collect from the rainfalls they receive. Grasslands are divided into two groups: temperate, which include prairies, and savanna. Although these almost treeless plains do not support as many animal species as the forest habitats, they do provide a plentiful supply of food for the animals that live on them. Deserts are characterised by extremely low amounts of erratic rainfall, however, they are not totally arid and support a wide range of wildlife. Reptiles cope well in the desert and are able to survive for a number of weeks on one kill. In contrast, wetlands have a diverse range of habitats from swamps and rivers to glacial lakes. Marine habitats are extremely diverse from icy polar seas to tropical beaches and the mighty depths of the world's oceans. The potential loss of these habitats is the over-riding threat to the world's animals.

Just as important as the habitats in which the animal kingdom lives, is the conservation of these precious lands. Conservation does involve an element of preservation, but this is not its only job. Conservation also means the management of both land and animal. In ancient Africa, Asia and Europe, conservation often took the form of protective laws passed down by various rulers. Today's conservation has its origins in two different sources. First, came the game laws and second, bird protection. These are actually at opposite ends of

the spectrum. Game laws were introduced initially to protect animals so that they could be hunted for food or sport by landowners. However, bird laws were introduced to protect birds and wildlife in general from gun-toting predators – this is what most people understand by conservation.

Whether it be a "big" cat, bear, spider, shark, stingray, jellyfish, viper or crocodile, dangerous species of the animal kingdom hold a great deal of fascination for many reasons.

Lions and tigers – although spotting a tiger is unlikely – are large, majestic creatures that exude power and domination. African lions and the American cougar are the most deadly to man. There has been a dramatic increase in fatal cougar attacks in the US in recent years – probably due to decreasing habitat and the increase in tourists visiting the North American wilderness.

It is not always a good idea to pretend to play dead when faced with certain bears – the black bear, for example, will rarely attack a human and even if it does, the best form of defence is to become really aggressive in return. Brown "grizzly" bears are actually large enough to kill an adult male with one swipe of its paw. This is probably only likely to happen if you startle it. This would be one good time to play dead – the bear is more likely to leave you alone. That one paw could disembowel or decapitate you. People are often misguided – so bear attacks are fairly common – and don't realise the savagery that can lie behind these seemingly "cuddly" creatures.

The red back spider sits quietly under outdoor tables and chairs in the gardens of Australia waiting for any threat to brush against them, or to get a little too close. But Australia's red back is only one of roughly 50,000 different species of spider and, although bites are rare, many of the poisonous types are not designed to kill. They merely want to give a warning to stay away. Many bites are particularly nasty and can give excruciating pain, but you would be unlikely to die, especially given the anti-venom available. The old and infirm, as well as the very young, are more likely to die from a spider bite than the average adult. It is important to deal with any spider bite quickly and with as little fuss as possible.

Unsuspecting surfers are often mistaken for a dolphin by sharks as they paddle their boards out to sea to catch a wave, but in truth, sharks have been given an unfair name. Statistically, it is more likely you will suffer an accident at home than be attacked by a great white.

A jellyfish that stings you has no brain and has not made the conscious decision to do so. Of the 2,000 or so species, less than 100 of them are considered dangerous to humans.

A bite from a poisonous snake is much more likely to kill a human than anything else in the animal world. Of the 2,700 species of snake in the world, roughly 450 are venomous. There are around 50,000 fatal bites each year. Like most other animals able to kill, snakes will usually only bite if surprised, threatened or provoked.

The death inducing roll of the crocodile is designed to disorientate the prey – it works – and if the crocodile in question has grabbed a limb to carry out the attack, it is more than likely that the limb in question will be dislocated, broken and at worse, severed. There are 12 species in this family with the Nile, North American and Estuarine being the most dangerous to man. While in the US, the protected American alligator can be just as deadly to man, although attacks are very rare.

Chapter 2

Big Cats

THE EVOLUTION OF THE "BIG" CATS, including lions, tigers and leopards, for example, can be traced back well over two million years. From fossil remains it was possible to form an overview of the relationships with today's "big" cats. Distant ancestry has left these species with fundamental similarities. However, there are differences with those built for speed over land and those who have agility in trees, to cats that hunt by day and those who are nocturnal.

Most of the wild cat species face the threat of extinction in one form or another and only intervention by man, including managing breeding pro-grammes, will halt their demise. At the beginning of the 20th century there were more than 100,000 tigers alone. Today, only around 6,000 remain. These numbers are also true for many other "big" cats and the future of these

species is now uncertain.

Contrary to belief that cats are solitary animals, communication is vital and social interaction plays a large part in their behaviour. Social organisation and territory are a major factor for mating and the rearing of young. While communicating between groups allows the prey-to-predator ratios to be managed effectively, conflict over prey does not benefit the species as a whole. Wild cats are primarily solitary hunters by nature, however, some species, notably the lion, have developed the art of hunt-

ing in social groups in order to max-imise success. All the cat species are car-nivores and very rarely eat plants. Their teeth comprise of large carnassials which they rely on for slicing meat into pieces suitable for swallowing. The tongue of a wild cat is roughened with rows of backward-pointing projections allowing the animal to scrape meat off the bone of its prey, which has usually been killed by a bite to the neck.

Cheetah

HAVING BEEN FORCED OUT OF their natural habitat in most of Africa and Asia, the cheetah can mainly be found in east Africa, living in open country where it hunts by day for gazelles and impala. Built for speed – it can run up to 58mph – the cheetah is unable to unsheathe its claws and so most attacks end with the prey escaping. Having run at such high speed, the cheetah is naturally exhausted. Its temperature becomes so high after a chase that it would be fatal for the animal to continue its pursuit. When a cheetah is successful in catching its prey, it will often rest for at least half an hour once the prey is dead. Most cheetahs kill their prey by tripping the escaping animal and then biting the underside of its throat to suffocate it. The cheetah may need to rest but instinct will induce a need to eat quickly to avoid having prey stolen by a stronger predator.

The cheetah thrives in vast expanses of land where prey is plentiful. But although not as resourceful as other wild cats, they have been able to adapt to a certain extent. In Namibia (where most of the cheetah population can be found), they survive in various habitats including grasslands, savannas, dense vegetation and mountainous terrain. Despite their confinement in east Africa, around 200 cheetahs were recently found in Iran and measures have been taken to protect them. There is a small chance that some cheetahs still exist in parts of India although this is unlikely. In its former habitats, the chee-

tah was often domesticated, particularly by the Ancient Egyptians and used for hunting. Today, about 12,400 cheetahs remain in the wild.

Cheetahs are built with long legs and a slender body. They have a long tail – up to 84cm – which usually ends in a white tuft and distinguishes this small

wild cat from the leopard, for which it is often mistaken. Its short, coarse tan coat designed with small black dots aids camouflage. With its small head and high-set eyes, it sports black marks from the corner of the eyes which run down the sides of the nose to its mouth which effectively keeps the sunlight from its eyes. On average, an adult weighs

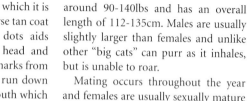

around 90-140lbs and has an overall length of 112-135cm. Males are usually slightly larger than females and unlike other "big cats" can purr as it inhales, but is unable to roar.

Mating occurs throughout the year and females are usually sexually mature around 20-24 months. Males are usually mature at 12 months, but do not usually mate until they reach three years old. Gestation is between 90-98 days and the average litter size is three to five clubs. Born with its characteristic spots, the cheetah cub weighs between five and 10 ounces at birth. Cubs also have underlying fur on their necks called a "mantle" which is shed as they grow older. This Mohawk appearance is probably designed to make the cub look like a different animal and so deter predators such as lions and hyenas, but death rates remain high during the early weeks.

Whereas male cheetahs are sociable and can group together for life, females are solitary creatures, living alone unless raising cubs. The first 18 months of life are extremely important and survival depends on knowing how to hunt while avoiding predators. After the first year and a half, the mother leaves the cubs. These cubs, however, will remain

together for a further six months where they form a sibling group. At two years old, female cubs leave the group while the males will remain together. In the wild, cheetahs live for up to 12 years and up to 20 years if kept in captivity.

Cheetahs are included on the IUCN (International Union for the Conservation of Nature and Natural Resources) list of vulnerable species as well as on the ESA (Ecological Society of America) list of threatened species. Founded in 1990 in Namibia, the Cheetah Conservation Fund is dedicated to the research, protection and conservation of cheetahs and promotes education to raise awareness of the plight of this wild cat.

Cougar

AMONG THE TOP PREDATORS IN North America is the cougar, sometimes referred to as the mountain lion, puma, panther or catamount. This one-coloured creature is extremely powerful with a large slender body, enormous feet and muscular limbs. Like the much smaller domestic cat, the cougar conceals itself while stalking its prey, lead-

ing to a surprise attack. With its short and coarse fur (usually grey or brown in colour), this ferocious creature can measure more than eight feet from nose to tail. In California, the cougar population is estimated between 4,000 and

6,000 and encounters with people are definitely on the increase. In the past, this large animal was more elusive and was quite happy to avoid the human population, but with its natural habitat threatened, cougars are increasingly leaving their familiar terrain in search of food.

With its shy and elusive nature, the cougar lives a solitary existence with males and females really only interacting for mating purposes when females are about 30 months old. Births take place all year round and litters of up to four kittens are usual. Born with dark spots, usually only one or two of the kittens survive staying with their mother for around 18 to 24 months, after which

they are on their own. Kittens weigh roughly one pound at birth and measure on average 30cm. They are weaned at two months and are then able to travel with their mother around the home range. The kitten's spots will fade after about eight to 12 months. During the time they spend with their mother, kittens will learn to hunt.

With their similar colouring to the African lion, cougars have a long and heavy tail which measures almost two thirds of the length of the total of this animal overall. Males are typically larger and heavier than females weighing around 110-180lbs, while females may weigh up to 130lbs. Cougars are renowned for their curiosity.

The cougar ecosystem involves this top predator maintaining a healthy balance in wildlife populations where deer are their primary food source. But cougars are opportunistic and will also feed on wild hogs, porcupines, raccoons, livestock, domestic animals, rodents, rabbits, hares, birds and even fish. Cougars are extremely versatile and – with their excellent vision, fast speed and ability to jump vertically up to 15 feet and horizontally up to 40 feet – their prey is unlikely to escape capture.

Cougars are naturally territorial and usually have a range that extends from 25 square miles to 1,000 square miles dependent on which part of North America they are based. The state of Texas provides its cougar inhabitants with the most space. Territories are marked with urine, earth and leaves. They are most often active at night but

this state has all but isolated the cougars in the Santa Ana Mountains. In effect, wildlife "corridors" have been blocked and unless they are opened up and the cougars are able to move and find new ranges then this particular group faces extinction. Equally, the damming of the Colorado River has led to a significant decline in the habitat of the desert mule deer giving rise to fears that the cougar here will soon have no prey. Many cougar populations that once existed are already extinct because of loss of habitat.

The chances of being killed or injured by a cougar is highly unlikely and in the past 100 years, only 14 fatalities have been recorded, however, it would be prudent to stay alert if visiting cougar habitats. For their part, cougars are more interested in unprotected livestock so farmers put their animals indoors at night. On the other hand, the more developments that are erected around the foothills of mountains, the more territory and habitat the cougars lose. In the US, various groups are trying to raise awareness so that man and the cougar can live side by side with the ever-decreasing space that exists between them.

can be seen at dawn or during twilight hours. As adaptable creatures, cougars are at home in a variety of habitats including the alpine forests of Alberta, the tropical areas of Mexico and Arizona's desert plains.

Cougars are facing trouble in other ways though. In the Santa Ana Mountains in California, the ecosystem is just not viable enough to sustain the wild cat population. Development in

Jaguar

JAGUARS TAKE THEIR NAME FROM the ancient Indian word "yaguar" which means "the killer who overcomes its prey in a single strike". Many people mistake the jaguar for the leopard. The way to tell them apart is by their rosettes. While leopards have plain black rosettes, the jaguar's rosettes are black with lighter markings inside them. The jaguar also has a much more stocky muscular body and shorter tail giving an almost pit bull-like appearance.

Found in the central regions of North (Texas) and South America (in countries such as Brazil, Paraguay, Peru and Mexico), these cats used to roam from

the southern states of the US down to the tip of South America. Primarily a forest dweller – they are particularly prolific in the Amazon – these creatures are also at home in grasslands and woodlands. Jaguars that live in more open terrain have lighter fur than those who live in dense forests and need the camouflage in the undergrowth of the forest floor.

Unlike leopards in the savanna who have to compete with the likes of lions and hyenas for prey, jaguars have no rivals. Depending on their location, jaguars are capable of hunting during the day and at night – although nocturnal traits happen in areas where jaguars live in close proximity to man. Whereas other cats will suffocate or sever the spinal cord of their prey, the jaguar has particularly powerful jaws and can kill with its teeth by piercing the skull with one bite. The size of prey also depends on what's available. In Belize, the armadillo is the most prolific source of prey, but jaguars do favour livestock, deer, monkeys, reptiles and even fish. They tend to inhabit areas close to a water source where fishing skills are useful. Jaguars are expert at this as well as being good climbers where they hunt

for monkeys in the lower tree branches. Unfortunately, jaguars are in competition with poachers and hunters who are looking for the same species as the "big" cat. Because of this, jaguars are frequently shot on sight despite protective legislation.

Jaguars are solitary and like other "big" cats mark their territory with urine and tree scrapes. From its meow to its roar, the jaguar has shown that it is active for up to 60% of the time in any 24-hour period. Female jaguars reach sexual maturity between two and three years, whereas the male is about three to four years old before reaching maturity. There is no defined breeding season for the jaguars and mating takes place all year round. Gestation takes roughly 100 days after which the female will give birth to a litter of between two and four cubs. Cubs stay with their mother who feeds and protects them for 12 months, although they stay with her until they are two years old. Life expectancy is 11 to 12 years in the wild, while in captivity, as with other "big" cats, they can live for more than 20 years.

During the 1960s and 1970s, around 18,000 jaguars were killed every year for their highly sort after fur. Thanks to leg-

decline. In Belize, with help from the World Wildlife Fund (WWF), 150 square miles of rainforest – the Cockscomb Basin Wildlife Preserve – provides a protected environment for roughly 200 jaguars. In other parts of South America, the WWF is also providing aid to protect some remaining rainforests which still provide a refuge for the majority of the remaining jaguar population. With many organisations protecting the jaguar, hunting is banned completely in Argentina, Brazil, Colombia, French Guiana, Honduras, Nicaragua, Panama, Paraguay, Suriname, Uruguay, Venezuela and the US. Brazil, Costa Rica, Guatemala, Mexico and Peru have some hunting restrictions in place.

islation and environmental pressure, this practice has declined dramatically, although they are still hunted today. Another huge threat for the jaguar is loss of prey and habitat from deforestation. They have had to move further from their forest habitats in search of food which effectively fragmented the "big" cat population and left them in isolated pockets in the Americas. Estimates put the number of jaguars left in the wild today at 15,000. Conservationists are working hard to re-establish their habitats and halt their

Leopard

THE LEOPARD CAN RUN AT JUST under 40mph for a short time, leap more than 10 feet vertically and 20 feet horizontally, is good at climbing and is also an excellent swimmer. Closely resembling its cousin the jaguar, the leopard is the second most powerful "big" cat in the world after its larger

cousin. Leopards vary in length from three feet to six and a half feet and are roughly between 17.5-30.5" tall. Males weigh between 80-150lbs, although some have been known to weigh a mighty 200lbs, while the smaller female weighs between 62.5-100lbs and is around two thirds the size of the male. Territories are marked similarly to other "big" cats with urine and scrapping earth.

Originally, the leopard was thought to be a hybrid of the lion and panther and this is where it gets its name. Where leopards are the primary predator, for example, in African rainforests or in Sri Lanka, they tend to be larger than other subspecies in the savanna, who compete for prey with other large predators including lions and hyenas.

This wild cat is particularly powerful and is distinctive with its spotted coat, short limbs, heavy torso, thick neck and long tail. A typical leopard sports short sleek fur which is usually a pale straw colour with black markings, known as rosettes. However, leopards do come in other colours including grey, chestnut and black. The latter are found mostly in rainforests. These creatures are particularly adept at surviving in almost any kind of habitat that provides them with enough food and water except central deserts including mountains, savanna and woodlands. Leopards are typically found in Africa, Asia, across the Arabian Peninsula and Korea. A black panther is a melanistic leopard which is a mutation that produces more black pigment than tan-orange.

It is estimated that there are around 500,000 leopards worldwide although they do face the threat of loss of habitat and increased hunting pressure. Under immediate threat today are the Anatolian, Barbary, North Chinese and South Arabian leopards.

Leopards sexually mature between two and three years and, after a 90-100 day gestation produce between one and three cubs. Leopards may mate all year round in Africa and India, but in Siberia, for example, the mating season takes place between January and February. Mortality for cubs is high. Mothers-to-be will find a safe place, usually a tree hollow, thicket, or crevice among boulders where she will make a den. From three months onwards, cubs start to follow their mother out to hunt. At around 13-18 months, the cubs become independent of their mother, although siblings typically stay together for several months following this. The animal will live for 10 to 12 years in the wild, while just over 20 years is the norm in captivity.

Renowned for being solitary animals, leopards are legendary for their camouflage skills and can move about near to human habitats virtually undetected. Mainly nocturnal, especially in areas where they themselves are hunted, they are opportunistic creatures that have an extremely flexible diet. From the small beetle to an antelope twice its own weight, this carnivorous animal also feeds on carrion which it will hide in trees – leopards are not good at defending their prey from other predators such as lions and hyena – and will return nightly to consume their meal. Leopards are fond of reedbuck, impala, gazelles, the young of larger species including

wildebeest and zebra but will also eat hares, birds and smaller carnivores. They will eat just about anything though and are known for eating monkeys, rodents, reptiles and wild pigs. With their strong hearing and eyesight, they are usually assured of a good meal.

Mostly leopards will avoid people, but it is not uncommon for a human to become targeted as prey. An injured leopard, or one struggling to find a usual source of food will invariably prey on humans and may find they have a liking for it. Two leopards in India, the "Leopard of Rudraprayag" and the "Panar Leopard" (in Kumaon), claimed over 125 and 400 lives respectively. Both were eventually killed by legendary hunter, Jim Corbett, in the early 20th century.

Lion

TWO JAPANESE TOURISTS VISITING Kenya's Masai Mara learnt that lions are not to be messed with…both sadly went home in a box. Although man is "on the menu", lions prefer medium to large sized herbivores in different ecosystems, including zebra, wildebeest, buffalo,

warthog, kob, impala, gazelle and gemsbok. They will, however, eat any species, which might include smaller mammals, birds, reptiles and rodents. They will also kill and eat other "big" cats including the leopard.

With good acceleration, but little stamina, it is important for lions to get as close to their prey as possible before charging. Stalking and camouflage are therefore crucial and lions mainly hunt

under the cover of darkness. A lion needs to be no more than 20-30 metres away from its prey before pouncing to be reasonably sure of a kill. Even when they do strike, the prey still has a fairly good chance of escape, unless it is young, old or sick. Lions usually kill by strangulation or suffocation while other prey are killed by more specialised techniques. This includes the buffalo. The buffalo herd may be followed for a long time while the lions show no attempt to stalk. It is believed that the

lions are waiting for the right time when they might panic the herd and so send buffalo in different directions making it easier to select and capture a prey. While warthogs, for example, are dug out of their burrows.

Lions exist in prides of around two to 18 related adult females (mothers, daughters, sisters and aunts) that occupy a territory. In areas like the Serengeti, female lions are active hunters while the males seem to merely hang around in order to mate and protect their young from other predatory males. However, in more wooded areas, such as the Kruger National Park, females have more shelter for their cubs and males and females tend to look after themselves and do their own hunting – and because the cubs are relatively better protected and not in the open, the males are more free to roam further looking for other females with which to mate. The fact that lions hunt in prides gives them a huge advantage over other "big" cats that are solitary. These social groups increase their hunting success by working together and this enables them to tackle larger prey than they would physically be able to do if they worked alone. However, solitary lions obviously have a higher food intake generally because they are not required to share their food.

Cubs are brought up and looked after by the pride and mothers synchronise the births of their cubs so that they can co-operate in raising each others cubs by suckling them and protecting them

from predatory males. Female cubs will usually stay in the pride for life, whereas male cubs will leave between the ages of two and four. These males then concentrate on feeding and forming coalitions. This helps them prepare to take over another lion's territory when they fully mature. Displacing established males of a pride is often a violent business. If the displacement is successful, the males of the coalition then commit infanticide in order to make way for their own cubs. If infanticide did not take place, new males would have to wait up to two years to sire their own cubs. Despite trying to stop their own cubs being killed the females are ready to mate within days of losing their offspring. The members of the coalition and members of the pride all have equal status. Gestation takes three and a half months and mothers produce between one and four cubs. More than 80% of lion cubs die before they reach two years of age.

Prides stay within a specific territory, covering 15 square miles, although when prey is scarce, it is known for a pride to travel over 100 square miles in search of food. Larger prides are renowned for bullying smaller prides and it is not unknown for a larger pride to kill their neighbours. With less than 200 in number, only the Asiatic lion in India is endangered. With the introduction of wildlife preserves in Africa, lions here are thriving.

Tiger

TIGERS ARE ONE OF THE BIGGEST and most fearsome predators in the world with a sleek body, padded paws, and muscular limbs. Its senses – particularly sight, smell and hearing – are all highly developed which, combined with its stealth, grace and cunning, makes it an exceptional hunter. Like all other "big" cats, tigers are carnivores.

With its distinctive golden body and black vertical stripes, the size and colour of a tiger varies according to the climate in which it lives. Male tigers generally weigh between 180-320kg, while the smaller female weighs in at 120-180kg. In 1967, the largest Bengal tiger that was shot weighed a massive 390kg. As a tiger becomes older (it has an average lifespan of around eight to 15 years) the stripes become more prominent and a female tiger always sports bolder colours than the male. The smallest

tigers are the Sumatran, while Siberian tigers are the largest. In summer, the tiger's colours are an effective camouflage and it is extremely difficult to spot a tiger hidden in undergrowth.

It is believed that tigers first came from Russia and then extended through Manchuria, Korea, China, Burma, Thailand, Vietnam, Malaya, Java, Sumatra and the island of Bali. Tigers

domestic cattle, wild pigs and deer, but they are known to kill dogs, leopards, pythons and young crocodiles. If necessary, they will also prey on smaller animals and birds. An injured tiger will attack a human, giving rise to the name of "man-eater", but this is relatively rare. Tigers only tend to do this if they are desperate and even a blow from its paw will kill a human. Although elephants are far too big and dangerous for tigers to kill and eat, they will attack on occasion. Even though it is bigger and heavier than other cats, the tiger can reach speeds of around 37mph and, unlike the lion who suffocates its prey, the tiger bites the back of the neck, severing the spinal column – although it will bite the throat of larger prey. Its forearms will then bring the prey to the ground and the tiger will remain attached to the prey's neck until it dies.

Tigers are territorial and defensive and females usually have a territory of 20 square kilometres. Adult males have a larger territory of between 60-100 square kilometres, which obviously overlaps those of the females. Tigers are by nature quite aggressive with each other and territorial disputes are violent. Males mark their territory with

then established themselves in Bengal, the foothills of the Himalayas – where they can be found at altitudes of 2,400-2,700 metres – and central and southern India.

Tigers are the largest and heaviest of the "big" cats and most live in forests or grasslands. They are particularly strong swimmers and are fond of bathing in ponds, lakes and rivers. They hunt alone and primarily eat medium to large sized herbivores including water buffalo, urine and secretions from their anal glands. Females are only receptive for mating for a few days, although mating may take place many times during this period. With gestation lasting just over three months, females will usually give birth to three or four cubs which they then raise alone. By eight weeks, cubs are ready to follow their mother out of the den, and they become independent by around 18 months. However, they will stay with their mother until they are at least two years old. Female tigers will stick to territory near their mothers while male cubs will wander much further afield.

The Bengal tiger or Royal Bengal tiger is the most prolific of all the subspecies of tiger found in the world today. Found in Bangladesh and India, it lives in various habitats including grasslands and tropical rainforests and is estimated to have a population of 4,500. Despite having the highest population of the subspecies, the Bengal tigers' habitat is under constant threat and immense measures have been taken to protect them. A project carried out in India – Project Tiger – increased their number and is today considered one of the most successful conservation pro-grammes in the world.

Despite our fear of them, humans are the tiger's biggest predator and they are often hunted illegally for fur and body parts used for medicinal purposes. In western Thailand, the Tiger Temple is home to tame tigers that walk around and are available for tourists to touch. Not bad for the world's strongest and most ferocious feline.

Chapter 3

Bears

UNLIKE ALMOST ALL OTHER DANgerous animals, bears can be found throughout the world. They are generally large in stature and tend to walk on their heels, like humans (plantigrade). Along with their large bodies, they have short legs, small ears, forward facing eyes and a stub for a tail. They are classified as carnivores but have a tendency to be herbivores to varying degrees. The giant panda almost exclusively eats plants.

Humans have always had, and still do, a great connection to the bear. The earliest known religions paid great homage to this large animal with bear cults and ritual burials of bear remains evident through nearly every culture in the world. In some cultures, the bear was so reverential that people were not allowed to even mention the word "bear" and a number of other words and euphemisms were created in many instances.

In ancient times, there was such a strong belief in the bear throughout Scandinavia, it was actually believed that some people had the power to change into or take on the characteristics of a bear – and the word "berserk" in English comes from this legend. A warrior who dressed in a bear skin that was treated with oils and herbs, it was believed, would gain more strength, stamina and power and be able to imitate the bear in battle.

Today, bears are greatly protected and, quite rightly, respect for them remains high. In British Columbia, Canada, there are around seven attacks a year on humans – mainly from the brown bear, or grizzly – where about one fatality occurs every two years. Starving bears are dangerous: the Sun Bear in Indonesia, usually passive, has begun to launch itself at people because of the reduction of food sources. However, if a bear stands on its hind legs, it's more likely to be taking a look than eyeing you up for lunch.

Asiatic Black Bear

THIS MEDIUM SIZED BEAR IS VERY

similar to its cousin, the black bear (they are thought to share a European ancestor), but unlike other bears, the Asiatic black bear has relatively large ears which seem out of proportion to its head. With a white patch of fur on its chest – often shaped like a "V" – this bear has not been as greatly studied as other bears. Despite its name, other colours of the bear are common, including white, brown and even a blue glacial bear. It possesses strong forearms and sharp claws which enable the bear to climb trees successfully. Other names for this bear include the Tibetan black bear, the Himalayan black bear or the moon bear. The bear has been quite prolific and successful and there are 18 subspecies to be found in the US and Canada. True numbers of this bear surviving in North America are not known, but estimates have been as high as 750,000.

Found also throughout Southern Asia, they live in countries such as Afghanistan, Pakistan, Nepal, Northern India, Bhutan and Burma, but they may also be seen in northeast China, parts of Russia, Taiwan and the Japanese islands, Honshu and Shikoku. Living in mostly forested areas and favouring hilly and mountainous terrain, in summer months the bears move higher up the mountains. During the autumn months, those who find their supplies of acorns and other food sources scarce are inclined to scavenge for food on farms where they kill trees and take corn. Those that moved higher up the mountains in summer months move lower down the slopes in winter to escape the cold. In more northerly parts these bears have dens in winter where they tend to sleep for around five months.

Their diet is particularly varied depending on the season. Asiatic black bears are partial to a variety of plant life and during the winter months fatten themselves on acorns, chestnuts and walnuts. Spring provides them with an abundance of plant life including bamboo, hydrangeas and raspberry plants. During the summer they will also take advantage of strawberries and grass, but they also eat insects – particularly ants – and bee's nests although they have been known to eat carrion and will if necessary attack livestock. In China's Wolong Reserve, the Asiatic black bear shares habitat with another cousin, the giant panda, where the staple diet consists of bamboo. Naturally, like all bears, they are particularly fond of honey.

With adults reaching an average length of four feet to just over six feet, males typically weigh between 240-330lbs with females weighing slightly less at between 140-200lbs. These bears do not normally breed until they reach three or four years old. In their northern territory bears breed in early summer where the young are then born in

their mother's winter den. However, in Pakistan, mating might not take place until the autumn. Cubs generally stay with their mother for two to three years. Females with first-year young do not usually breed the following season. The bear's life expectancy is roughly 25 years, although they may live to 30 years in captivity.

Renowned for being more aggressive than the black bear, the Asiatic black bear is more likely to attack a human and there are numerous records of fatal attacks. These attacks are likely to be as a result of the bear having been startled.

Loss of habitat through deforestation is also largely to blame, although farmers defending livestock also play a part in their demise. Another threat involves the bears being hunted for the bile in their gall bladders which is used for medicinal purposes. China outlawed the poaching of native bears during the 1980s so special farms were set up where bears are kept caged and catheters are inserted to remove the treasured bile. Supporters argue that without these farms the bears will once again be persecuted by hunters, however, critics maintain that this is an extremely cruel and inhuman way to keep the bear and

that a synthetic substitute would work equally as well. The Asiatic black bear is listed as "vulnerable" on the World Conservation Union's (IUCN) Red List of Threatened Animals.

Black Bear

THE BLACK BEAR CAN STAND between four and seven feet high and has much shorter claws than that of the grizzly, or brown bear, allowing it agility when climbing trees. Front claws are used for climbing and keeping a hold and females will often encourage their young into the trees in this way if there is danger. A common characteristic of almost all bears are their small round ears which are slightly more tapered. With a shaggy coat and small eyes, the black bear is smaller than the grizzly and has a less concave face. The black bear is known by other names including Kermode bear or cinnamon bear and is found in North America (although a small population exists in Mexico).

Found in forests in Florida (and northern Mexico), to Alaska and Canada, the black bear is also at home, and is safe, on the open tundra in northern Labrador now that the grizzly bear no longer roams there. Although called the black bear, like many other bears, colours may vary and some have a brown or blonde coat. There are even

white black bears in British Columbia in Canada. Like its cousin, the Asiatic black bear, the number of bears surviving in the wild is estimated at 750,000.

Males are typically larger than females and average between 125-500lbs depending on the season, food available and the bear's age. Females usually weigh around 90-300lbs. Mating usually takes place from late May to early July, although this can be extended to August in certain ranges. Most bears are aged between three and seven years when they start mating. Cubs are born in January or February and a typical litter will have two to three young each weighing roughly between a half to one pound. They stay with their mother for around 17 months and up to a week before mating begins again, when the mother will encourage the cubs to become independent. Black bear mothers have never been known to kill a human in defence of cubs. Much of the black bear's life depends on the food sources available. For example, a female will typically wait two years before mating again and having another litter, however, if food is in short supply a mother will abort her own foetus and wait for three to four years to have another litter. Black bears live between 21 and 33 years on average. With more males being killed by humans than females, the ratio of the species is typically one male for up to five females.

Black bears are efficient hibernators and lose body heat extremely slowly which allows them to sleep for up to seven months while effectively cutting their metabolic rate in half. Their bodies remain at temperatures above $88^{o}C$ (which is within $12^{o}C$ of their normal summer temperature). In the more southern states, where food is plentiful all year round, some bears don't hibernate at all. In order to prepare themselves for hibernation, bears typically feed on nuts, acorns, fruit, insects and succulent greens. Meat, such as small mammals, deer and livestock, is really only eaten by black bears when preferred foods are not readily available. In their forested habitat, with deciduous and coniferous trees along with streams, swamps and rocks, bears prefer the thick vegetation of the forest floor with its abundant food sources. These mature forests provide soft and hard mast in summer and autumn while wetlands are particularly important for providing new plants during the spring.

Black bears have quite a large brain in relation to their head size and are renowned for being one of the more intelligent mammals. With an excellent long-term memory these bears are also able to understand a simple concept. They are known to be good swimmers and can swim more than one mile in fresh water and lighter bears can run in

Brown Bear "Grizzly"

AS ONE OF THE LARGEST LAND-based carnivores, a brown bear – or grizzly as they are often called – can weigh between 290-1,550lbs. Due to regular feeding and less exercise, some brown bears in captivity weigh up to 2,000lbs. Found throughout the northern hemisphere, the brown bear also includes the subspecies of the Kodiak and Mexican brown bears. With its furry brown coat – with a range of shades from blonde to black – the brown bear has a large hump of muscle across its shoulders that gives it incredible strength. This, combined with powerful forearms, gives the bear the ability to dig as well as the sheer force to break the neck or spine of an adult buffalo with a single blow. They sport massive paws which have claws of up to nearly six inches in length. Unlike other large predators, bears are unable to retract their claws.

From head to toe, brown bears average between five feet six inches to over nine feet while some Kodiaks can reach more

excess of 30mph. Bears are active before dawn, and sleep again soon after sunset – although they take a nap during the day. This does depend on location and some black bears are active at night in order to avoid people and other bears.

than 10 feet. With a great deal of stamina, brown bears can reach speeds in excess of 35mph and are capable of running at full speed for miles without stopping.

Native to Asia, Europe, North America and the Atlas Mountains in Africa, at one time, many are now extinct or have suffered vastly decreased populations. They live predominantly today in British Columbia, Alaska, the Yukon and northwest Territories as well as Idaho, Montana, Wyoming and northwest Washington. There are an estimated 200,000 brown bears living in the wild, with the largest population of 120,000 existing in Russia. More than 32,500 can be found in the US while Canada reportedly has nearly 22,000 bears. Much smaller populations can even be found in Mexico. The brown

bears in the Pyrenees between France and Spain numbered about 15, but females were in such short supply that in 2006 bears from Slovenia were released into the wild to maintain the balance in the region. However, in Arctic areas brown bears are on the increase. Due to global warming the area is considerably warmer than it once was and this potential habitat is attracting bears further north into what used to be exclusively polar bear territory.

Like tigers, bears ambush their prey when hunting which they will nearly always kill with a sharp bite in the neck using their huge canine teeth. Bears are resourceful and, as well as hunting prey, they are also drawn to food sources generated by humans, including rubbish dumps and litter bins. They are inquisitive and will search barns – even people's homes – the closer man builds to the bear's natural habitat. Bears themselves like semi-open country with mountainous terrain – by walking on rocks while being hunted themselves these bears can retrace their steps and avoid their predator. Their diet is a mix of plants, berries, fish, insects and small mammals, including squirrels. More than 90% of the brown bear's diet is actually vegetable matter and their jaw structure has evolved to reflect this. Brown bears are good at fishing and in both Russia and Alaska they feed mostly on salmon – which probably accounts for their enormous size.

Brown bears, although aggressive in nature, actually got the nickname "grizzly" from the lighter colour on the tips of their fur, this is called "grizzling". Although bears will attack humans – particularly mothers with cubs – there are relatively few serious incidents and usually only one or two fatal attacks

January and March. Cubs stay with their mother until they are around two and a half years old and have a life expectancy of roughly 20-25 years.

Giant Panda

WITH ITS HIGHLY DISTINCTIVE black and white coat, the giant panda is probably the most misunderstood of all the bears. For many years it was considered to be a type of racoon, like its cousin, the red panda, but genetics and observation revealed otherwise and it was eventually, in 1995, recognised as a member of the bear family. It has a very large head in relation to other bears and in fact is virtually a herbivore with more than 98% of its diet being bamboo. This is quite interesting because pandas lack the enzymes to efficiently digest bamboo and they gain very little in the way of energy or protein from it. They consume between 25-35lbs of bamboo a day. Pandas also have an interesting number of differences to other bears. They have six digits on their front paws, giving them a thumb and five fingers. This is ideal for holding bamboo stalks, while the male genitalia is rear pointing and

each year in regions such as North America. Attacks will usually occur when the bear is particularly aggressive – when it's been injured or is sick – although in Scandinavia there have only been three reported cases of fatal attacks in the last 100 years.

These bears reach sexual maturity between four and a half and seven years, although some males do not become successful breeders until eight to 10 years old because of older rival males. Mating takes place between May and July and litters with one to four cubs are born between

small – not at all in line with other bears.

The giant panda can only be found in six regions in southwest China including Sichuan, Gansu and Shaanzi provinces as well as Tibet. With high altitudes ranging between 4,000-11,500 feet, these areas cover less than 5,400 square miles in mountain forests which are home to more than 30 types of bamboo. Pandas' territories are entirely dependent on the abundance of bamboo. Territories of males generally overlap those of several females and like other bears the giant panda is thought to be a solitary creature unless it is a female with cubs. However, recent studies show that small groups of pandas do get together outside the breeding season.

Male pandas average between 190-275lbs and are around 64-76 inches in length. Typical of all bears the females are slightly smaller and lighter. Pandas reach sexual maturity between four and a half and six and a half years and mate once during the spring. Females give birth to cubs in August or September and on average have one cub – although litters may contain up to three cubs. Weaned at nine months, panda cubs generally stay with their mother for around two years. Life expectancy is from 20-30 years for those living in captivity. There is little known about life expectancy in wild pandas. Pandas mark their territory with urine, scratching trees and by secretions from their anal glands.

After the poaching and hunting of the 1930s and 1940s in China, the giant panda was under immense threat. Non-Chinese were not allowed to kill pandas, although locals continued to hunt this animal for its soft fur. The panda's habitat was declining rapidly after the Chinese population boom in the late 1940s and famines led to increased hunting. The Cultural Revolution saw all conservation efforts halted and after Chinese economic reform, illegal poaching continued in order to supply Hong Kong and Japan on the black market. As a result of the demise of the giant panda throughout the early 20th century, the Wolong National Reserve was set up by the PRC in 1958, but it was not until the 1990s that conservation was totally understood and effective. So rare and adored are these creatures that their natural habitat was declared a UNESCO World Heritage Site.

Loss of habitat and documented low birth rates – although recent studies show that giant pandas reproduce as well as the brown bear – all put the giant panda under constant threat. Killing a panda was punishable by death in China until 1997 when the law was relaxed and offenders can now expect to spend 20 years in prison instead. There are an estimated 1,600 giant pandas in the wild and it is an endangered species, however figures show that in contrast to other wild bears, numbers of pandas are actually on the increase. In addition, scientists in 2006 believed that this estimate was too low and that numbers in the wild may even be as great as 3,000. Giant pandas are often considered docile, however, they have been known to attack humans, but it seems as if this is more out of irritation than because of a predatory nature.

Polar Bear

THE POLAR BEAR IS THE MOST CAR-nivorous of all the bears, however it is also the most patient. A mighty hunter of seals, it will sit by a blow-hole for hours waiting for the animal to surface. With one powerful blow from its paw, the polar bear flips the entire seal onto the ice. Once a seal has been captured, the polar bear bites its head and neck before dragging it several metres from the water to feed. First, it eats the skin and fat then it eats the meat. They stop often to wash during feeding either by using water or rubbing themselves in the snow. Despite their size, polar bears often don't eat their entire kill and this enjoyment is left for other bears, arctic foxes and gulls. This enormous animal is the largest land-based carnivore. Found throughout the Arctic, polar bears are incredibly nomadic in their search for prey which – along with the ringed seal – includes bearded, hooded and harp seals as well as a young walrus.

With harsh conditions and tempera-tures virtually always below freezing the polar bear has had to become an expert survivalist. The hairs on the body are

actually translucent – not white – and the skin is black, enabling the bear to soak up the sun's rays so it can glean some warmth from the harsh condi-tions. Just like other bears, the polar bear's ears are round. They are even smaller than those of other bears and lie closer to the head. Despite their massive bodies, polar bears are excellent swim-mers, helped by their enormous paws being slightly webbed. They can swim

for several hours over long distances, propelled by their front paws while their hind feet and legs are held flat and act like rudders. Most polar bears can be found around landmasses on the edge of the polar basin. Although they have been known to travel as far up as the North Pole, scientists believe that they are not frequent visitors as the northern Arctic Ocean has little food.

In years with heavier ice, the bears have travelled as far south as Newfoundland and Iceland.

Male bears grow up to three times the size of females and weigh between 772-1,450lbs with a length of nine feet. Females weigh between 331-551lbs and reach sexual maturity around four years of age while for males it is generally two years later. Breeding takes place during April and May on the sea ice. Gestation is eight months and like other bears there is a delay in implantation of the fertilised egg. This delay ensures that the cub is born at the best time of year for survival. Most mothers prepare a den around October, which is usually dug out of a snowdrift. Cubs are born from November to January and first emerge from the den in March or April. Most litters have two cubs and a litter of three or four is quite rare. Polar bears nurse cubs for up to 30 months when they are then deemed independent. Mothers are extremely protective of their cubs. Most adult females give birth once every three years so competition for breeding females is fierce among the males. Life expectancy is between 20 and 30 years, but only a small proportion actually live more than 18 years.

Polar bears are most active first thing in the morning and if they're not hungry can often be seen sprawled on the ice taking a nap later in the day. On cold days the bears curl up and cover their muzzle area and have been known to excavate temporary dens to keep warm. Male bears do not hibernate – only pregnant females are known to do this. They are mainly solitary, however groups of bears have been reported congregating especially in some southern regions.

Human and polar bear habitats overlap and unlike other bears, the polar bear does consider humans as prey.

Consequently, the person attacked will be killed by the bear, unless the bear is killed first. Younger polar bears and females with cubs attack more often – unfortunately these bears also visit rubbish dumps and towns more often than others to scavenge because they are hungrier and thinner.

Chapter 4

Crocodiles, Lizards, Alligators & Hippos

ALLIGATORS, CROCODILES AND THE Komodo dragon are all extremely hostile to humans, but it is the hippopotamus that will kill the most by far.

In Africa the hippo is heralded with the title of being the country's mammal responsible for most human fatalities. The hippo is not a hunter. It is a large herbivore that only attacks if threatened in its own territory. However, it is this fact, combined with the hippo's ability to run much faster than a human that makes it such a danger.

The frequency of alligator attacks on humans is increasing. In the US, there were only nine fatal attacks between 1970 and the end of the 1990s. However, there were more than 11 human deaths by alligators between 2001 and 2006. Although alligators are naturally scared of humans, those who believe they are safe have a misguided false sense of security and it is probably this that has led to more deaths in five years than there were in the previous 30 years.

Of the 12 species, the Nile, North American and Estuarine crocodiles are the most dangerous due to their large size. Attacks usually take place when crocodiles are protecting themselves, territory and the nests of young. They are prone to hunger and will eat people, however humans are not their preferred choice. But often, an attack by a croco-

Alligator

THESE LARGE, SEMI-AQUATIC REP-tiles have a huge tail – which accounts for half their length. The tail has many uses which is why it is so large. It is used as a weapon and stores fat to nourish the creature during the winter months. It also acts as a propeller when the alligator is swimming and is used to make "gator holes" during dry seasons. There are just two types of alligator.

The American alligator can grow to a length of up to 19 feet (although the average length is 13 feet) and it weighs roughly 800lbs. The Chinese alligator grows to just six feet. Alligators are distinguishable from crocodiles by their broad snout and are often darker in colour, sometimes appearing almost black, although this is dependent on the water in which the alligator lives. Water with more algae produces greener animals, while water with overhanging trees produces more tannic acid giving the alligator a much darker skin. They can achieve different speeds depending on whether they are walking in a belly crawl, a high walk or gallop. When swimming, alligators can reach speeds

dile will happen purely because it has a bad attitude. Estuarine crocodiles are renowned for being particularly bad tempered. If you want to escape an alligator or crocodile, run away in a straight line. Running at 20mph, the creature will out run you for roughly 10 metres, but after that it needs a rest. If you are in water, the alligator or crocodile will be looking forward to you as its next meal.

of around 10 kilometres per hour.

In the US, alligators can be found in Georgia, Florida, Alabama, Mississippi, Louisiana, Texas and along the coast of the Gulf of Mexico. The majority of the alligator population is located in Louisiana and Florida (numbers here are estimated to be in excess of one million). The Chinese alligator is rare and is an endangered species found along the banks of the fresh water Yangtze River basin in China although experts are now predicting long-term survival. In an attempt to preserve this species, the Rockefeller Wildlife Park in southern Louisiana has a number of Chinese alligators in captivity. In the US, alligators are adaptable and can be found living in wetlands, marshes, fresh water rivers and ponds.

Alligators are nocturnal and therefore feed mainly at night. Adults will eat other reptiles, mammals, fish, turtles and birds which they swallow whole. Younger alligators tend to stick to small fish, frogs, tadpoles, insects and snails. Although this reptile has around 80 teeth, they are simply used to catch prey not to tear it apart. They are opportunistic feeders and will eat carrion or other, younger alligators if they are hungry enough. Larger prey is caught by the alligator's teeth and, if too big to consume in a single bite, will be taken to water where the reptile can drown it. This type of prey – including humans – is then allowed to rot or the alligator spins the prey until bite-sized pieces are torn off – this is known as the death roll. However, alligator jaws are relatively weak and it is possible for a strong human to hold the reptile's mouth shut with bare hands. Unlike larger crocodiles, alligators will not instantly see a human as prey.

Breeding takes place between April and May and mating rituals are noisy. Unlike most other predators, alligators do not need to reach a certain age to sexually mature. This maturity usually depends on the size of the reptile.

Around 28 days after mating the female lays around 30 eggs in a large nest which she has constructed of mud, leaves and twigs. Rotting vegetation in the nest – which is roughly three feet tall and six feet wide – is used to warm the eggs as the female would crush the eggs if she lay on them. It is the temperature in the nest that will determine the sex of the baby alligators. If eggs are warmed in excess of 93ºF the embryos develop into males. Between 86ºF and 93ºF both sexes develop, while below 86ºF produces females. It is the mother's job to protect the eggs from predators. Eggs take two months to hatch and hatch-

lings are roughly nine inches long. Alligators are among the most nurturing of reptiles and the pod – as hatchlings are known – stay with their mother until they are around 12-24 months old. Life expectancy is around 15 years in the wild.

American alligators are protected by law and anyone caught feeding the reptile will be heavily fined. A special patrol service was set up to help those living in close proximity to alligators to deal with any problems that might arise.

Crocodiles

CROCODILES ARE INCREDIBLE SURvivors. They evolved around 200 million years ago and managed to survive when the dinosaurs faced extinction, outliving them by 65 million years. Many of the crocodile fossils found today show that this aquatic reptile has changed very little since its evolution. However, there is evidence of crocodiles with hooves and those that were mainly land-based. Their successful survival may be in part due to the fact that they are renowned for being vicious hunters and are extremely adaptable.

Like alligators, crocodiles nurture their young and grow into huge creatures capable of facing a lion and killing a large zebra. Five species of crocodilia are endangered today, the Philippine, Siamese, Orinoco, Tomistoma and the Chinese alligator. No crocodile species have become extinct – even in the past 200 years or so when man's impact on the animal kingdom in general has been extremely detrimental. Crocodiles are also quick to learn how to avoid dangers. They can also sustain terrible injuries. During territorial fights it is common for the reptile to tear off the legs of an opponent. These heal and animals are often found in the wild with missing limbs.

Crocodiles vary in colour from grey-green to dark olive to greyish-brown while their back is ridged with bony scales. Adult males weigh up to 450lbs and measure from seven to 15 feet in the larger species of the American crocodile, while an enormous salt water reptile can reach more than six metres long and weigh in excess of 1,200kg. Crocodiles have 66 teeth – used for catching prey – and when lost grow new ones.

Crocodiles are found throughout the world and live in the tropics in Africa, North America, South America, Australia and Asia. There are both fresh and salt water crocodiles whose habitats include lakes, ponds, rivers, wetlands and marshes as well as coastal areas.

Despite the historic appearance, crocodiles are highly advanced and are extremely successful predators. With their streamlined bodies and webbed feet they are fast swimmers. Crocodiles are ambush hunters, lying in wait for mammals or fish to come too close at which point they rush and grab the prey. They are able to survive long periods without food and rarely need to actively hunt for their meal. They have an incredible bite which is capable of killing other large predators including lions, tigers and even sharks. But despite their exceptional predatory skills if their mouth is held shut they lack the strength to open it again.

Incredibly, the small Egyptian Plover feeds on parasites that are found in the mouth of the crocodile. The reptile will open its mouth for the bird to feed from and clean out the parasites. Like the alligator, they will eat other, smaller members of its own species.

Female crocodiles lay eggs in a large hole. Eggs are laid almost two months after mating. During incubation the mother is vigilant and only leaves the nest to swim. Males stay close by to intimidate predators. When the hatchlings are ready they cry out once they've broken the shell with their "egg" tooth. The female digs out the nest and removes the eggs from it with her mouth. Sometimes she will roll the eggs around on the ground to help the young hatch. In larger species, females lay between 25 and 80 eggs, while smaller species lay between 10 and 15 eggs. Hatchlings remain with their mother for up to three years. Although many are

eaten by adult crocodiles – especially when populations are healthy – if a hatchling does mature, life expectancy is between 50 and 60 years.

The salt water and Nile crocodiles are responsible for killing hundreds of people each year in parts of Asia and Africa. However, wild crocodiles are protected by law in many parts of the world, but they are also farmed commercially for their hide which is used to make leather goods. Their meat is considered a delicacy in some countries and is served pickled. Crocodile meat is white and, while nutritious, is generally higher in cholesterol than other meats. The most common crocodiles to be farmed are the Nile crocodiles and salt water species.

Hippopotamus

WATER DEEP ENOUGH TO LIE HALF-submerged in is an absolute must for the hippopotamus – which means "river horse". Submersion of this semi-aquatic mammal keeps the animal's hairless skin from overheating and prevents this thin layer from dehydrating. These enormous mammals prefer a water source that is gently sloping and has a

firm bottomed bed. This environment also allows females to nurse their young without the calves having to swim. Despite its size, the hippo is able to move with grace under water, although it is not typically buoyant and so uses its short back legs to propel itself off the bottom of the river or lake in particularly deep water.

Hippos are greyish brown in colour on the top of their bodies, while the underneath is a pale pink. They have a broad mouth that can be opened incredibly wide and their large canine teeth are used in aggressive displays both with other animals – particularly crocodiles with whom they usually share rivers and lakes – and adult males threatening their territory. Teeth are not just used as a threat though and are the hippo's main weapon should a fight ensue. A hippo's ears, eyes and nostrils are found on top of its head which allows it to remain submerged in water while maintaining its senses enabling it to stay alert to dangers and, of course, to breathe. An adult male will weigh between 1,600-3,200kg and be between three and five and a half metres in length. Females are smaller and usually weigh between 655-2,344kg. They have

a short tail that measures around 55cm.

Today, hippos are found in the Sudan, Kenya, areas of the Congo and Ethiopia as well as Uganda and the Gambia, Botswana, Zimbabwe, Zambia, Tanzania and Mozambique where the largest populations live. Not strictly nocturnal, hippos like to forage for food – grass – at night so that they can spend their lazy days socialising, digesting food and sleeping. Although their main diet is grass, hippos have been known to scavenge carrion.

In the water, hippos are social creatures that stick together in herds of around 10-15 however, herds can number 50 or more where water is in short supply, but when looking for food they are solitary. The exception to this rule is females with their young. Herds are typically made up of a dominant male, females and young and adult males control their territory with intense aggression. Male hippos reach sexual maturity between seven and nine years while females reach maturity slightly later at eight to 10 years. Hippos can mate all year round, but seasonal birth peaks coincide with peak rainfall. Gestation lasts for around 240 days after which time the female gives birth to a single

calf. Calves remain with their mothers for many years and many females will have up to four calves that she is looking after at any one time. Particularly young calves will be guarded by a number of females in a "crèche" while their mother takes other young out to forage for food. Life expectancy for a hippo in the wild is up to 40 years.

Like many other animals, the biggest threat to their survival is the loss of habitat – particularly where man has started to encroach on the animal's territory because of population growth, increased development and technological advances. Another major threat is illegal hunting and poaching. Hippo's meat is sought after and skins and teeth – which can measure up to 60cm – are also highly valued. However, some farmers are suspected of shooting the animals illegally because of the threat of hippos raiding crops. The animal is notorious for this and causes extensive damage by grazing and trampling on crops. It is possible for farmers to file a complaint with officials that will eventually lead to the animal's demise, however, some farmers make false claims in an attempt to be pro-active and eliminate the threat of destroyed crops while others take matters into their own hands. In addition, the ban on international trade in elephant ivory has led to increased demand for the teeth of hippopotamuses. In particular, in the Democratic Republic of Congo, hippo populations have been decimated through hunting. Where once there was a population of 25,000 of these large mammals, today there are just 2,000 left in the area.

Komodo Dragon

AS AN OPPORTUNIST EATER, THE Komodo dragon will eat small and injured humans and human corpses. During the 20th century more than 12 human deaths were attributed to this lizard. They are carnivorous and cannibalistic and have a huge appetite, consuming vast quantities in a relatively short amount of time – they can eat up to 80% of their own body weight in one meal. It has been reported that an average dragon can eat a quite large pig in less than 20 minutes. Other meals include small deer, other reptiles,

smaller dragons, monkeys, other mammals and birds although if necessary, the dragon is capable of attacking and killing an adult water buffalo. Komodos bite their own gums when they eat, resulting in blood-like saliva which creates a culture ideal for bacteria that live in their mouths – even if prey does escape the jaws of the Komodo, the bacteria will lead to infection and certain death later for the victim. The dragon, using a keen sense of smell will then be able to locate the prey – sometimes from up to four miles away. The Komodo can stalk its prey before reaching speeds of up to 12mph in order to finally catch it. The dominant male eats first followed by other dragons when he is finished. Females eat together although other than this they are mainly solitary. Flesh is torn from the prey while the Komodo holds down the victim with its front legs.

The Komodo dragon is the largest species of lizard and grows to around 10 feet with a tail that is as long as its body. A large adult can weigh around 200lbs and has up to 60 teeth that can reach one inch in length. These are serrated and designed to tear prey apart while its flexible skull allows the Komodo to swallow large pieces of food. Like other lizards, the

Komodo has a long snake-like tongue and skin colour varies from grey to red in males while females are an olive green.

Found in central Indonesia, Komodo, Rinca, Flores and the smaller islands of Padar – which does not have a permanent population – Gili and Montang, Komodos have a total range of less than 1,000 square kilometres. Natural habitat is harsh with a rocky arid landscape where water is in short supply for most of the year. Localised flooding is common in the monsoon season and most Komodo dragons are to be found in forests, the savanna and grasslands where they prefer the dry open landscape. The Komodo is most active during the day and is an excellent swimmer. The young are capable of climbing trees – to avoid the dangers of predators and Komodo adults – by using their front leg claws.

Males fight over females for breeding by grappling on their hind legs. The dominant male pins the loser of the fight to the ground. Komodo dragons mate between May and August with females displaying signs of resistance to start with. Eggs, of up to 20 at a time, are laid in September in the ground or in tree hollows and have an incubation of seven months. Many hatchlings do not survive. Young dragons take up to five years to mature and life expectancy in the wild is around 30 years. Like some other reptiles, a female is capable of parthenogenesis – self-reproduction. This phenomenon may be attributed to the fact that Komodo dragons do not reproduce readily.

Today, there are estimated to be 3,000-5,000 Komodo dragons in the wild where the largest threat to their survival is their habitat where volcanic activity – including fire – reduces the lizard's numbers of prey. Man is the adult dragon's only predator and the poaching of skins is illegal under CITES – the Convention on International Trade in Endangered Species. As the dragon is an endangered species, the Komodo National Park was founded in 1980 to enable conservationists to protect the reptile. There are current concerns that there are less than 500 breeding females left in the wild and the dragon is also protected on the IUCN Red List. This list provides specialist information on conservation, taxonomy and distribution and is designed to determine the relative risk of extinction of the species.

Chapter 5

Sharks, Rays & Other Fish

ON THE SUBJECT OF WHAT CON-stitutes a danger in the sea, most people will instinctively think of sharks, however, there are many creatures that live in the tropical oceans of the world that can give you a nasty or fatal bite or sting.

Despite the menacing teeth of the barracuda, attacks on humans are rare. Like many other predators, this fish will usually only attack if provoked or startled. Meanwhile, there are around 100 species of jellyfish capable of injuring a human. These invertebrates eat mostly zooplankton that they capture with toxic tentacles whose lengths vary from several inches to 100 feet long. Travelling around the ocean on self propulsion with winds and tides they

survive in tropical and cold oceans and seas. The sea wasp, or box jellyfish, is one of the most deadly stinging species in the sea.

Piranhas, like sharks, have an unfair reputation for biting and maiming humans and attacks are exaggerated. However, it is not wise to dangle limbs in waters of their native habitats – shoals are likely to attack, especially if hungry and although piranhas in captivity will eat flake food, wild species of the fish are mainly carnivorous.

Although a number of species of shark are powerful predators and are capable of killing a human, many species will actually swim away. When encountering a shark and in order to

avoid an attack the most proven way to get out of the situation with your life (and hopefully limbs intact) is to move toward the creature and maintain a calm exterior.

Stingrays have barbs along the spines on their tails which can sting like a scorpion. These act as both a deterrent to predators and a weapon in the case of attack.

Barracuda

THE BARRACUDA IS CAPABLE OF growing up to six feet or more and despite its fearsome appearance does not really deserve the label it is sometimes given as a predator of man. It will be the sudden movement of a swimmer unaware that erratic moves are likely to startle the fish, that may cause a fatal bite. However, a barracuda will stop after taking a bite of a human as they are not the usual or preferred food source.

Its long body is roughly about one foot wide and is fairly compressed with small smooth scales. The jaw of a barracuda is powerful with the lower jaw jutting out underneath the upper while the mouth comprises strong fang-like teeth. Its colour varies from green to grey on top of its body, while underneath the fish is much lighter and fins tend to be a shade of yellow. The fish's gills do not have spines and the dorsal fins are set fairly wide apart while its tail fin is forked. The head is large and often looks pike-like in appearance. In Hawaii, the barracuda is also known as a kaku.

Found in the tropical and sub-tropical oceans of the world these fish predominantly live in the waters of the Atlantic, and the Indian and Pacific oceans. They are a fascination for underwater photographers, scuba divers and swimmers and unprovoked attacks on humans are rare. Renowned for being scavengers, some will follow a diver. It is thought that the fish believes the diver is a large predator that might capture and leave a prey behind that the barracuda can then have the remains of. However, despite the rarity of attacks on humans, its reputation as a vicious, ferocious, hunter is well-founded. Victims of the barracuda include young barracuda, bream, snapper and other fish that eat plankton such as groupers. Attacks are swift and the barracuda charges its prey at high speed – the fish

can swim up to 27mph – taking a large bite with its jaws. Sudden movements and bright light underwater will quickly engage the fish's attention and alert it to potential prey. Although the barracuda relies heavily on its eyesight to find prey, if it is in murky waters, it will often attack before identifying what it's attacking. Barracudas hunt alone if they are larger species while smaller species hunt in groups. A group will often swiftly move a shoal of prey closely together and towards more shallow water to maximise success. Some schools of barracuda exist together in numbers of several thousand. In some areas of the world barracudas are found to be poisonous and this is attributed to the types of poisonous fish that they feed on.

Little is known about the location and spawning of the larger barracudas, but it is known that they do not care for their young. Young barracuda are known to stay together and this is in part for protection. It is also not known how to tell a male and female barracuda apart and there is also no sure way how to tell how old an individual fish actually is although it has been documented that life expectancy extends up to 14 years.

Hunted as game and as food they are most often prepared for eating as a fillet or steak and have a strong taste like tuna. However, barracudas are not highly prized on the dinner table and most are caught for game fishing. When caught, the barracuda puts up a good fight on the hook, and often leaps out of the water in an attempt to escape. But this large fish has little stamina and quickly tires. Larger barracuda have to be fished in deep waters with cut bait. Curious by nature, the fish will often follow a fishing boat for up to a thousand feet.

The barracuda is not considered to be nocturnal, unlike some of its close relatives, however, both solitary and groups of barracuda have been spotted in the water on nights when there is a full moon and it is believed that this is the fish taking advantage of being an opportunistic hunter. But generally the fish rest at night and are usually only awakened by the lights of night divers. There are 26 species of barracuda including the Sharpfin barracuda, Guinean barracuda, Pacific barracuda, Great barracuda and Sawtooth barracuda.

PIRANHA

PIRANHAS ARE A GROUP OF FRESH water carnivorous fish that live in the rivers of South America, although they do belong to the sub-family Serrasalminae which includes closely-related herbivorous fish such as pacus and silver dollars. In addition, a type of herbivorous piranha can be found in the Maroni River which is known to host colonies of worms in its stomach.

Normally about 15-25cm in length, piranhas are known for their sharp teeth – which can bite through a steel fishing hook – and have a renowned aggressive appetite for meat and flesh. Normally only found in the rivers of the Amazon, Guyana and Paraguay, they are also spotted occasionally in the Potomac River, however, the colder environment here does not usually sustain their survival. Piranhas are found in the warmer still lakes or slow-moving streams.

Piranhas have a high-backed stocky body with a large head. Telling a male and female apart is extremely difficult. Its teeth are hidden behind its lips and

are difficult to detect. Even a young piranha, only six inches long, can inflict serious injuries with its teeth which are roughly four millimetres long.

Piranhas have never been introduced, either by accident or intentionally, in any other part of the world and most of the piranha populations inhabit "whitewater" rivers, so called due to their great numbers of fine particles that give the water a milky/yellow/grey appearance.

Other piranhas live in "blackwater" and "clearwater" rivers in temperatures of between 24-30ºC. Piranhas probably only exist in South America due to Pororoca which is a phenomenon that only happens in the rivers of the region because of their relief conditions. Pororoca occurs where the low altitude of the river – the Amazon is only 150 metres – means that the sea tides clash with the fresh water and in its increasing resistance of the salt water a compressed mass of water "explodes" causing waters to rise to between six and eight metres, thereby creating a giant wave that rolls towards the ocean. The Pororoca leaves the river abundant with the animals killed during the process and it is the piranhas ability to "clean-up" this environment by scavenging on the remains that keeps the eco-system in the region healthy and without disease.

The normal diet of piranhas consists of fish, carrion and sometimes river vegetation. Although natives of South America are known to swim in piranha infested waters where attacks are rare, it is not recommended to swim during the drought season when the fish are much more aggressive due to food shortages. But at other times, shoals of piranhas will actually swim away from humans and current thinking is that piranhas congregate together for protection rather than to hunt. However, these shoals can also be highly dangerous. Their razor-sharp teeth are capable of stripping anything and everything if they are hungry enough – including much larger animals – in a matter of minutes or even seconds.

When the water levels fall dramati-

cally during the dry season, food is scarce. Piranha infested waters are usually safe at night when the fish are asleep, but unfortunately, this is the time when other predators also dangerous to humans are hunting including caimans – a member of the crocodile family. Humans are always advised to avoid piranha territory if they have an open bleeding cut. They are able to sense blood in the water and are much more likely to attack a larger animal if they think it is injured or dying. However, it has recently been discovered that piranhas are more likely to attack if there is a great deal of commotion in the water than if there is blood. A shoal of hungry piranhas is capable of inflicting serious injuries on humans and can even cause death.

Spawning usually takes place before the rainy season in April through to May – although it is thought that further spawning may take place in late summer. Prior to spawning, piranhas become more aggressive and pairs defend spawning territory while preparing a "nest". A large number of eggs are laid which hatch after two or three days (depending on water temperature). Both parents protect the eggs and the young fish – which would otherwise be easy prey for other piranhas.

In their local environment, piranhas are renowned for being delicious and are a popular food.

Sea Wasp or Box Jellyfish

THE SEA WASP, OR BOX JELLYFISH as it is also known, is probably one of the deadliest sea creatures found in the oceans around Australia and the Philippines. Although not all species of sea wasps are dangerous, the vast majority of this invertebrate has venom which is often fatal. In 200 years, sea wasps have claimed the lives of more than 5,500 people making it one of the most dangerous species known to man. However, their venomous spit is not designed to kill humans and it is actually a form of defence as well as a device to stun prey prior to ingesting it.

Most human deaths are caused by the larger variety known as Chironex fleckeri which has a high concentration of nematocysts. These are cells on the outer part of the jellyfish which sting prey by injecting a toxin. Some of these are toxic to man. Turtles, interestingly, are not affected by the toxins of these jellyfish and regularly eat them as part of their diet. Sea wasps can be avoided on clear, calm days as their semi-transparent forms are not too difficult to see, but during the wet season, coastal waterways are often flooded, muddy and turbid which makes them a great hazard to fishermen.

Numerous deaths still occur around the north Queensland coast of Australia where the potent poison has been known to kill a child within minutes of being stung. The pain from the venom of these invertebrates is excruciating and increases very rapidly. Where tentacles and skin have contact, large brown/purple welts appear making the victim look as if they have been whipped. Death is caused by shock to the heart, complete circulatory failure and respiratory paralysis. Adults can also die within minutes if not treated extremely quickly. Venom attacks human red blood cells and damages the skin where the poison has penetrated. Today, there is anti-venom available but it must be administered immediately. In the absence of anti-venom and immedi-

ate medical assistance, applying vinegar for a minimum of 30 seconds disables the nematocysts that have not yet reached the blood stream. Tentacles should be removed from the skin as quickly as possible following application of vinegar. Also, cardiac arrest can happen extremely quickly following a sting from the sea wasp so it is advisable to carry out CPR on the victim.

From November to May sea wasps are abundant in the waters however scientists are still divided about where they disappear to during the winter months. It is known, however, that sea wasps sleep on the ocean floor between 3.00pm and dawn where it is believed they conserve their energy and avoid predators. Some experts believe that sea wasps actively hunt their prey. If they do, they are fairly effective hunters able to move quickly with speeds of up to

three and a half knots – instead of drifting as a "true" jellyfish would.

In addition, they have 24 eyes at the centre of each side of their bell which occur in clusters on four sides of their cube-like bodies. Most of the sea wasp's eyes are simple, however, one pair in each cluster is much more complex containing a lens, retina, iris and cornea. Scientists have proved that sight is blurred. What is also a mystery is how the jellyfish processes its visual information. It does not have a brain and nervous system, although it does appear to have four primitive organs which might be a form of brain.

Instead of a true nervous system, jellyfish have a nerve net which allows them to detect light, odour and other stimuli in the form of receptors. Sea wasps consist of an outer layer and an inner layer which lines their gut. Between these two layers is a thick jelly-like substance called "mesoglea" or "middle jelly". The one opening acts as both a mouth and anus for the jellyfish which has a simple gullet, stomach and intestine. A number of arms are found located at the mouth to help transport food from the tentacles to the opening. The male or female reproductive organs originate in the gut lining. Embryonic development takes place during which larvae are formed. These become polyps which divide and form into young jellyfish known as ephyra. This process takes several weeks and the life expectancy of the sea wasp is three to six months.

Shark

SHARKS EXISTED LONG BEFORE the dinosaurs, and like crocodiles, have managed to outlive these prehistoric creatures by around 65 million years. Sharks are a type of fish that live in waters the world over, in every ocean and even some rivers and lakes. They have no bones and are made of cartilage – a tough, fibrous substance – nowhere near as hard as bone.

There are numerous varieties of sharks that range in size from five or six inches up to 50 feet long, although most are slightly smaller than this and, of the 368 or so species worldwide, half are actually less than 40 inches. They come in a variety of body shapes although most are streamlined, enabling them to glide seemingly effortlessly through water. The angel shark which lives on the ocean bed is fairly flat allowing it to hide under sand, while others have an elongated body such as the cookiecutter shark. Saw sharks have a long nose and hammerhead sharks have a wide flat head while thresher sharks have a huge upper tail fin which it uses to stun its prey.

Like other predators, sharks do not chew food but gulp it down whole in quite large pieces. Their teeth can number up to 3,000 in larger sharks and these are arranged in roughly five rows which rather than being attached to the jaw are embedded in their flesh. Upper teeth are used to cut prey while lower teeth are largely confined to holding prey. Like alligators and crocodiles, if a shark loses a tooth it is replaced fairly quickly by the growth of a new one. Front teeth are large and carry out most of the work. Although sharks vary enormously, most comprise a rounded body which leads to its head and snout while the other end of the fish has a caudal fin or tail fin. Like other fish, sharks have two dorsal fins and pectoral fins. Sharks respire with five to seven gills.

Bony fish use a gas-filled swim bladder for buoyancy. The barracuda is known to have an extremely large bladder for this purpose, however, sharks rely on a large liver – sometimes the liver constitutes 25% of their body mass – which is filled with oil, but effectiveness is limited and sharks sink when they stop swimming. They rely on their superior sense of smell to find prey and are attracted to chemicals found in the gut of many species. In the Pacific Ocean, sharks feed on sea lions, seals, pelicans and the occasional diver. Attacks take place relatively close to the shore and often sharks mistake surfers "swimming" on their boards for prey. It is known that they swim underneath the prey and then launch a

lightning vertical attack.

During the 20th century, there were 130 shark attacks along the Pacific coast of North America with California receiving the most attacks (a total of 111) between 1950 and 2005. Ten of these were fatal with the great white being the most likely suspect.

There have always been a high number of fatal shark attacks along the coast line of East Asia, this region has the highest fatality rates in the world at 54%. The last fatal attack took place in September 2000 in Miyako in Northern Japan. However, Papua New Guinea suffers the worst attacks and has had nearly 70 incidents. Despite official documentation of authenticated shark attacks, it is believed the number is far higher than recorded as records in these areas tend to be unreliable and shark attacks are obviously not good for tourism.

In Australia, according to records, over the past 200 years, South Australia has seen the highest number of shark attacks – the last of which was in 2005 – with 12 attacks overall, nine of which were fatal. New South Wales suffered the next highest number with 10 attacks and seven fatalities. Western Australia and Victoria have seen eight and six

attacks respectively, although of the three fatalities in Victoria the last one took place in 1958. There have been four fatal attacks in Western Australia, while in Tasmania, of the four recorded attacks three have proved fatal. Queensland has reported three attacks and only one was fatal in 1992. Between 1990 and 2005, South Africa reported 72 attacks, while Brazil and Hawaii reported 62 and 57 respectively.

Stingray

RELATED TO SKATES AND SHARKS, the stingray is a marine fish made of cartilage which is common throughout the world's tropical waters. These graceful swimmers festoon the ocean floor where their sandy brown colour protects them and acts like camouflage while they dig for crabs, shrimp, worms and clams. The stingray is shaped rather like a diamond and its mouth is positioned on its white under belly, making it ideal for feeding along the bottom of the ocean. Fresh water varieties can be found in parts of Africa, Asia and Florida and most species are not threatened or endangered.

Stingrays are generally thought to be dangerous, however, they are unlikely to attack aggressively or defend themselves, preferring to swim away from predators and inquisitive species. The shark is the stingray's main predator and the barbed stinger in the tail is virtually useless for protection against

their mighty cousins, however, it will give a human a nasty wound. If stepped on, the stingray's tail is whipped up usually stinging a human on the foot. The stinger is likely to break off in the attack, but does no harm to the ray. It just grows another. However, the sting from a ray can cause pain and swelling in humans caused by the actual cut and the venom released. It is also possible to get an infection from any of the stinger left in the wound. Stings lead to punctures, severed arteries, poisoning and on very rare occasions, death.

Unfortunately, the only way to treat a wound from a stingray is with extremely – almost scalding – water which eases the pain by breaking down the venom. An immediate injection of anaesthetic around the wound will help, bringing the victim instant relief. Pain from a sting can last for several hours and is accompanied by fatigue, headaches, fever and nausea. However, stingrays are often fairly docile and, if you're spotted, the ray is much more likely to swim away rather than wait to sting. However, since the death of Australian television presenter and naturalist Steve Irwin in late 2006, stingrays have received a bad press. The presenter was punctured in the chest by a stingray while snorkelling. Of all the attacks by stingrays to the chest, half have proved fatal. However, this is an unusual display of stingray behaviour and this type of "puncture" attack is very rare.

Stingrays swim by propelling themselves along using their enormous pectoral "wings". This can look like underwater "flying". Some stingrays are no bigger than a human hand, while others can reach six feet in diameter and have a length of up to 15 feet. Stingrays can be solitary, although they can also be found living in pairs or in groups. Mating takes place during the winter months where the male follows the female biting her pectoral disc to see how receptive she is. Live young are born in groups of between three and five and females look after their young. Stingrays are beset by parasites that are drawn to the mucus on their skin. Spanish hogfish, reef fishes and bluehead wrasse "clean" the stingrays by eating these parasites. Other fish will also follow stingrays as they swim around the ocean floor as skimming along kicks up many other creatures for the ensuing fish to eat.

Stingrays lie on the ocean floor lying in wait for their prey. From underneath the sand where they hide it is not possible for the ray to see its prey. It relies on its sense of smell and electro-receptors to determine its next victim. The stingray's diet is made up of molluscs and crustaceans and sometimes, small fish. It possesses a powerful mouth with strong teeth which are capable of crushing shells.

Despite the dangers that these creatures can hold for man, they are a fascinating marine fish that divers and snorkellers are keen to see. Found in shallow sandy waters, in certain parts of the world, stingrays can be seen in abundance. In Antigua and the Cayman Islands it is possible to feed stingrays by hand and in the islands of Tahiti it is possible to hand feed both stingrays and sharks. These popular tourist resorts are known as "Stingray Cities".

Chapter 6

Snakes

SNAKES ARE NOT OFTEN A FAVourite for many, but they are fascinating creatures all the same. Little is known of the origins of snakes which is in part due to their delicate frames not fossilising particularly well, however, one of the earliest snakes to appear in fossil records Lapparentophis defrenni dates from around 130 million years ago. A younger, semi-aquatic snake, Similiophis, which was found in North Africa and Europe, shows fossils dating to about 100 million years ago. Both these types of samples were miss-

ing the majority of the skeleton, however, they did provide experts and scientists with some idea of the evolution of these reptiles.

Reptiles, pre-dinosaurs, included the group known as Diapsids. This group was responsible for the dinosaurs and eventually for the modern lizards and snakes that we see today. The snake is, interestingly, an evolutionary cousin of the Tyrannosaurus and Triceratops. Around 10 million years ago, vipers as we know them today, were found on the planet. They were followed by pit vipers who developed heat sensors on the front of their faces allowing them to find warm-blooded prey at night. Then, about seven million years later, pit vipers developed a structure at the end of their tails – comprising of interlocking skin – which could be rattled to ward off predators.

Many people enjoying the wilderness do so safely and rarely see poisonous

rocks unless you are sure that you are out of a snake's striking range. Improve your knowledge of the wildlife in the area that you wish to visit. Always give snakes a wide berth.

Anaconda

AS ONE OF THE LARGEST SNAKES in the world, the semi-aquatic Anaconda is impressive to look at and can reach lengths of more than 29 feet. As a constrictor it inhabits the tropics of South America and has teeth and a powerful jaw which it uses to effectively hold onto its prey. Like crocodiles and alligators, the anaconda drags its larger prey into the water to drown.

It is also a heavy snake and an Anaconda measuring 20 feet will weigh considerably more than a 33 foot python. With an average weight of 550lbs and a diameter of more than 12 inches, this snake is truly enormous with females far out-weighing the males and the species includes green anacondas and yellow anacondas. The green anaconda fits in well to its wet, dense vegetation habitat, while the yellow has black spots and a unique pattern that

snakes. However, it may be impossible to avoid being bitten. There are some simple steps that can help travellers significantly lower the risks. These include sticking to designated paths and leaving snakes alone when one is spotted. Wearing long trousers and leather boots can also minimise risk. It's advisable not to pick up wood for fires or to move gives individual snakes a form of identification. There are also dark-spotted or Deschauense's anaconda and the Bolivian anaconda. Dark-spotted anacondas are found in northeast Brazil, while the Bolivian anaconda was only recently discovered in Bolivia in 2002 and is still being studied.

Typically these snakes have a large head on which its eyes and nostrils are positioned in order to allow breathing while it's mainly submerged under water. If away from the water for a considerable time, the anaconda is prone to ticks which attach themselves to its body. The snake is not as fast on land as

it is in water and it is capable of staying underwater for up to 10 minutes. The anaconda is not poisonous and is usually found in rainforests, savannas and grasslands as well as scrub and deciduous forests. Time on land is usually spent basking in the sun or resting in shallow caves and hollows. They are more likely to be found in slow moving rivers and swamps than fast flowing rivers and are active mostly at night. There are unconfirmed reports of giant anacondas existing in the tropical forests and rivers, however, many of these are unsubstantiated and sightings of 60 foot snakes are often regarded as exaggerated.

Lying in wait for prey, anacondas position themselves submerged in water or in branches of trees overhanging water. The anaconda's diet consists mainly of rodents, deer, fish, turtles, sheep, dogs and caiman, although it also likes birds, tapirs and capybaras. They have been known to prey on jaguars, although jaguars will also prey on anacondas. Other threats include large caimans and other anacondas. Young anacondas feed on smaller prey including frogs, mice and smaller rodents such as rats.

The anaconda has been known to attack humans, although fatal attacks are relatively rare. In order to kill its prey, the snake bites with its teeth and then locking its powerful jaws onto the victim, drags it into the water. As a member of the boa family, the anaconda is more than capable of squeezing its prey to death if it does not drown straight away. It does this by squeezing tighter each time the prey breathes out until the prey is no longer able to breathe in again. This method is relatively quick and then the snake is able to eat its prey whole, head first. With a jaw able to unhinge, the anaconda can swallow prey that is much larger than its mouth and while it eats, the muscles throughout its body contract in wave-like movements to move the prey further down.

Anacondas are generally solitary snakes that remain within their own territory, but the start of the monsoon season sees the beginnings of mating where courtship may last several months. Sexual maturity is reached in both sexes at around three to four years old. Females ready for mating give off pheromones to attract nearby males. After mating, gestation takes around six months after which live young numbering between 20 and 40 and measuring around two feet are born. Like other predators, anacondas fall prey to other species when they are very young. If they do survive this period, they grow rapidly for the first few years of life and have a life expectancy in the wild of around 30 years.

Cobra

COBRAS ARE VENOMOUS SNAKES that mainly inhabit the desert regions of Africa and Asia. Unlike vipers, cobras

are unable to fold their fangs down and so they tend to be shorter. Cobras grow on average to just over eight feet while the King cobra is the largest venomous snake in the world and may grow to 16 feet or more. The scales of a cobra look quite shiny, however, they are smooth to touch and – as with most species of snake – aid locomotion. The cobra's vision is limited at a distance, however movement is quickly seen and its sense of touch is acute.

These snakes will only usually attack humans if threatened or provoked. However, there is usually one fatality each year from a King cobra bite and this powerful snake has even been known to attack and bring down an elephant. The cobra has a fairly slow strike, particularly compared to other venomous snakes and the number of strikes that miss the potential victim is relatively high. However, cobra bites are fatal in around 10% of attacks on humans and all strikes that don't miss the victim should be treated immediately and considered potentially fatal. Anti-venom for cobra bites is now effective and the number of deaths has fallen dramatically, particularly in Asia. However, cobra bites are still one of the oldest fates of man, especially in this region. The recognisable "hood" – the skin and muscle behind the snake's head – is used to great affect fooling potential predators into believing the snake is bigger than it actually is. The hood works by elongating ribs that extend the loose skin around the neck.

There are various species of cobra including the spitting cobra – native to Africa – that is capable of spitting venom into the eyes of predators, the black cobra – found in Pakistan and North India – as well as the King cobra.

The spitting cobra can spray its venom up to a distance of eight feet. This causes temporary blindness and pain. Colours of this snake vary from pink to black. Another type of spitting cobra is the ring-hals from South Africa which is fairly small and only reaches around four feet in length. It is dark brown or black and has pale rings on its neck.

The Egyptian cobra is found along the north coast of Africa and is often referred to as an asp. All cobras grow each year and shed their skin. King cobras live a solitary life smelling with their forked tongue and feeling vibrations around them. As a cold-blooded reptile, these snakes keep to the same

temperature as their environment. Female King cobras lay between 20 and 50 eggs in a nest in early spring. Incubation takes up to 70 days and nesting females are highly dangerous, although the young are immediately self-sufficient upon hatching. Life expectancy for cobras in the wild is around 20 years.

Cobras are sometimes considered to be one of the most dangerous snakes in the world. Renowned for their intimi-

dating behaviour, including glaring eyes, darting tongue and hissing, cobras release a nasty toxin which affects the nervous system of its prey. The neurotoxin that the snake releases through its virtually hollow fangs paralyses the prey and suffocation occurs when the heart and lungs stop. Cobras are excellent hunters who move with stealth after their prey. The powerful bite can kill in seconds and its typical diet includes insects, lizards, frogs, rats and mice.

Food is swallowed whole, head first, ensuring that the legs of the prey are bent backwards and therefore slide more easily into the snake's mouth.

Although the snake kills an animal weighing roughly between six and eight pounds, it will only eat around a quarter of this prey. The rest of the animal is left as carrion for vultures and other animals to eat. Cobras attack their prey quickly, however, they have been seen to stay back, making no noise, and watch the prey as if it's falling into some kind of trap that the cobra has set. Food is not chewed and so strong acids in the stomach break down the food for the snake to digest. After swallowing a large animal – which can take hours – the King cobra, for example, can go without another meal for months.

Rattlesnake

RATTLESNAKES ARE NAMED FOR the rattle at the end of their tail which is used to warn larger animals – including people – of its whereabouts so that it can be avoided. This venomous snake belongs to the family of pit vipers and is found in North America including Texas, Oklahoma, Kansas, New Mexico, Pennsylvania, Alabama and Georgia. This reptile is extensively exploited in the US and is often traded without regulation or consideration. Of the 30 or so species of rattlesnakes, several are on the verge of extinction despite desperate attempts by conservationists to halt their decline. These snakes play an important role in the eco-system and by preying on rodents keep their populations in check. This helps limit crop damage and the spread of disease. They are also important as prey themselves to raptors and other animals. The timber rattlesnake, for example, is endangered or threatened in several states, but there is currently no legislation to protect the species.

Most rattlesnakes actually have weak venom when compared with that of a true viper or cobra, however, most species of rattlesnake have toxic venom that destroys tissue and is responsible for degenerating organs and disrupting the clotting of blood. Permanent scarring is likely from a rattlesnake bite and if not treated quickly an attack can result in the loss of a limb if treatment is ineffective in any way. This could lead to the bite becoming fatal. Anti-venom

greatly reduces the chances of death and of the 8,000 bites received in the US each year, less than 15 are fatal.

The Mojave rattlesnake has a powerful neurotoxin that paralyses its prey, which can lead to the victim's heart and lungs being affected, while the western and eastern diamondback rattlesnakes can produce enough venom to kill two or three humans in one go. The western diamondback, in addition, is also more than ready to defend itself in any situation. Most rattlesnakes will give their prey a full dose of venom, although the snake can control how much venom it delivers. This may happen when the rattlesnake is not intending to bite or is just giving a warning. It is estimated that of all the rattlesnake bites received, one-third are actually "dry" bites where no venom is released. However, on the whole, rattlesnakes would rather avoid humans than give an unsuspecting tourist a bite. Even if the snake does bite it is done in defence and is not an act of aggression.

Rattlesnakes have the ability to strike from any angle, even when they are on the move and can effectively inject venom from almost all positions. They do not need to take the time to form a coil before they strike. They are even able to bite under water although striking is more difficult in water pressure. It is only when the rattlesnake feels that they cannot escape danger that they will form a coil. This gives them their most effective strike with a stabbing lunge at the potential danger. Equally, this stance will be adopted for catching prey.

When a rattlesnake is first born it has a small rounded tip on its tail called a pre-button. Just a few days after birth, the young snake will shed its skin and will gain a button on its tail with the new skin. This button becomes the new segment of the rattle and no noise will be produced until another segment is added. Each shredding of skin produces another segment, however, more than nine segments is unusual on a wild rattlesnake. This is due to damage and general wear and tear encountered by the snake during its life. Vary rarely, if the tail structure has been permanently damaged, the rattlesnake can be found without a rattle at all.

What started as a misguided attempt to rid areas of rattlesnakes in the form of rattlesnake roundups, is now a commercial event which promotes animal cruelty and damages the environment. Organisers of these events argue that roundups are necessary to rid the landscape of rattlesnakes. However, conservationists and animal welfare authorities disagree. Conservationists are trying to educate the American public to understand that rattlesnakes play a vital role. They aim for people to give the snake respect and to leave them alone to continue with their important ecological functions.

Vipers

VIPERS BELONG TO A FAMILY known as the Viperidae. These venomous snakes can be found worldwide except in Australia and Madagascar. Vipers belonging to the sub-family Azemiopinae are found in Tibet, China and North Vietnam. Those from the Causinae family are unique to Africa, while Crotalinae species can be found across Eastern Europe, Asia, Japan, Taiwan, Indonesia, India and Sri Lanka,

from southern Canada to Mexico and in southern South America. The more common Viperinae is found in Europe, Africa and Asia.

Their long-hinged fangs are folded back against the roof of the mouth where each rests in a soft membrane of skin. When the snake is about to strike, maxillary bones rotate the fangs forward ready for action and the venom ducts empty venom from special glands into the fang. Vipers have an unlimited supply of fangs and behind the maxillary bone is a series of replacement fangs in progressive stages of development. Replacement fangs are put in place around every 60 days and each maxillary bone has sockets for moving fangs forward and holding current fangs in place. The whole process of biting takes very little time and is designed both as a method of catching prey and as a means of defence.

Nearly all vipers have a stocky body and short tail and because of the position of the maxillary bones and the venom glands they sport a triangular-shaped head. Vipers are predominantly ambush predators who hunt at night.

Like cobras and rattlesnakes, the viper is capable of causing severe dam-

age when it bites. The venom is designed to affect the heart, the clotting of blood along with excruciating pain and local swelling at the bite wound.

Vipers usually produce proteolytic venom which has two functions. First, vipers typically have weak digestive systems and the venom it produces has strong enzymes for breaking down its prey and aiding digestion, and second, the venom is used in defence.

As with all snake bites, a strike from a viper should be taken extremely seriously and medical attention should be sought immediately. These strikes are not always fatal, but if a bite is left unattended for too long, complications may ensue and an affected limb may even be lost. However, depending on the type of viper that attacked, the amount of venom that was injected and the size of the victim, less serious side-affects are more common. Vipers are the pinnacle of venomous snake evolution with the Gaboon viper probably being one of the most impressive. At more than seven feet, this viper has fangs of more than two inches long. Renowned for being somewhat docile, this snake is happiest on the forest floor in rainforests across central Africa where it successfully camouflages itself. Despite its highly toxic venom which it produces in vast quantities, there are very few reported deaths from this snake although it is capable of hunting and eating a small antelope.

The puff adder is greatly feared in Africa although death rates are relatively low. The saw-scaled viper, also known as the carpet viper, is responsible for more deaths than the Gaboon viper or the puff adder. In some areas inhabited by this snake, fatal bites happen in more than 80% of cases and a fatal dose of venom can be inflicted by a small snake less than 12 inches long. The European adder is capable of causing death, however, this is extremely rare and the snake is renowned for its placid nature.

The bush viper of Africa is a particularly predatory creature that is highly poisonous. Bush vipers are mainly tree-dwelling, nocturnal hunters whose colours range from pale green to brown and red. This predator usually hangs by its coiled tail from a tree and then ambushes its unsuspecting prey. There are many types of other vipers and sub-families. Most vipers are nocturnal, however some species such as the green pit viper and the Ceylonese palm viper – both common in Sri Lanka – are extremely active by day. Most vipers eat a varied diet and this usually consists of amphibians, small mammals, lizards, rodents and birds. Female vipers lay up to 20 eggs during August and mothers guard their young well. However, once the young snakes hatch they are immediately self-sufficient.

Chapter 7

Spiders

PERHAPS THE MOST FEARED OF ALL species of the animal kingdom are spiders. These tiny creatures bring dread into the hearts of many whether they are common household spiders that actually carry out a great deal of good in our homes, or are of the poisonous variety including funnel-webs, red backs and black widows to name but a few. The tarantula, despite its scary appearance, is the only creature featured in this book that is incapable of killing a human, however, it too has its dangers. Whatever fascination spiders hold for us, there is also an inexplicable fear of these arachnids which in many cases is not completely unfounded.

The initial bite from a spider may just be the start. Swelling and itching is common after a bite, but depending on the type of spider that has given the bite, there may be a variety of other symptoms to worry about. Spider bites need to be completely cured which involves treating both the bite itself and the side-affects. Correct ointments are the first step as these stop the swelling. Antibiotics and other medicines may also be necessary and will stop the risk of infection. In cases where a powerful spider bite has been given by a larger species urgent medical attention is a pre-requisite as anti-venoms will almost certainly be necessary. As with snake bites, it is important to keep the victim upright and the bite site lower than the heart. This helps to slow down the spread of poison. One cure that seems to work with both spider bites and, interestingly, jellyfish stings is the papaya fruit.

A traveller trekking around Papua New Guinea was bitten by a small spider. At the time it wasn't painful but the

bite soon developed into a gaping wound. The hole got larger and larger and no amount of cleaning, ointments or antiseptics worked. Eventually a papaya was used to plug the hole. It dried up within 12 hours.

Black Widow Spider

THE BLACK WIDOW SPIDER HAS two main body parts like all other spiders; the cephalothorax – which bears the head and legs – and the abdomen. The abdomen is much larger and houses the spinnerets which allow the spider to spin its web. On a black widow, the spinnerets look rather like a cluster of cones. Its web is a tangled mess and the black widow lives in a small portion of the web where it detects the vibrations of incoming prey including insects and occasionally woodlice.

The black widow belongs to the widow family of spiders of which there are five different species including the brown widow and the red widow. All are

found in North America. However, black widow spiders are found throughout the world. Generally though, most people refer to the three main species found in North America. These are the southern black widow, the northern black widow and the western black widow. In South Africa, for example, widow spiders are also known as button spiders.

Females are typically larger than male black widows and an adult female can have a body length of around half an inch and a total leg span of roughly one and half inches. Gravid females – those carrying eggs – are generally larger than other females and can have an abdomen which is larger than a half inch in diameter. Males by comparison are almost half the size of females. Males may also be totally black in colour or may maintain some young spider colouration and they usually sport some red markings on the top or underside of the abdomen. Young spiders have a completely different colour to adults and are generally grey with white stripes with some spotting of yellow and orange.

These spiders prefer dark, quiet spots outdoors including crevices, however, if they do venture indoors they are likely to be found in basements and attics rather than in kitchens. They are a particular pest in commercial properties and businesses, such as warehouses, where they weave webs between walls and stationary objects.

Mating takes place during the spring.

Females lay their eggs in a spherical silk sac and each egg sac contains between 200 and 300 eggs. Each female is capable of producing between four and nine egg sacs during one summer. The young widow spiders hatch around eight to 10 days after they are laid from the eggs during which time they molt and then wait at least a further two weeks before they emerge from the egg sac. Generally, there is only one generation of widow spiders each year.

The name widow spider came from the untrue belief that females ate male widow spiders after mating. It is now known that under research conditions males were left with females after mating and were probably mistaken by the female for prey. Subsequent studies have shown that females rarely eat the male after mating unless for any reason he has been unable to leave her web.

The black widow does not damage property, however, they cause fear in

some people that come into contact with them. Although these spiders are not renowned for being aggressive they do occasionally bite humans. This usually happens when the person brushes against the web and sometimes females guarding eggs will bite, although they often flee instead. The venom of these spiders causes a condition called latrodectism. Like snakes, this venom is neurotoxic and attacks the nervous system. Initially, a bite may go unnoticed, and the first symptom might be when the victim feels a dull numbing ache around the bite mark. This can lead to painful muscle cramps, particularly in the stomach, and may also lead to nausea, other muscle cramps, sweating, raised blood pressure, heartbeat irregularities and vomiting. A peak in symptoms usually takes place between one and three hours following the bite and these are usually gone within 12-24 hours. However, in less than one per cent of victims, a bite from a black widow spider can be fatal. As with other venomous spiders – including the red back in Australia – the old, infirm and the very young are at most risk and are likely to experience more severe symptoms.

Brazilian Wandering Spider

WANDERING SPIDERS IS THE TERM used to describe the Ctenidae family of spiders. Although the spider's range is known to stretch beyond Brazil – where they were first observed – the group is commonly called the Brazilian wandering spider. The spider is fairly hairy and has spindly-looking legs which can span up to five inches or more. With their strong legs, aggressive nature and their distinctive red jaws which they display when angered, these spiders are known to bite more humans than any other spider in the world.

These fast, aggressive spiders are extremely venomous, large in size and are ranked among the most dangerous spiders known to man. The Brazilian wandering spider is often found in homes across South America and likes to hide in shoes, hats and other pieces of clothing. As its name suggests, the wandering spider prefers to wander about the forest floor – when not hid-

ing in someone's footwear and does not weave a web in which to catch prey. It is an active hunter that inflicts intense pain on its victim.

Also known as the banana spider because of its ability to remain undetected hidden among bunches of bananas bound for other countries, this spider deserves the utmost respect.

However, the use of the name banana spider should not be confused with the banana spider of North America which is harmless.

Found among the tropical and subtropical regions of South America, the Brazilian wandering spider is a land-based nocturnal hunter who likes to feed on crickets, large insects, small

aggressor and waits for the right moment to strike. The spider is able to leap almost two feet in order to attack its prey or an aggressor. On the forest floor, the Brazilian wandering spider is likely to be hiding under logs, trees and generally dark places, however, the spider can also be found in banana trees and palm trees as well as construction materials and the furniture (as well as clothing) in homes.

There are around five fatalities from this spider's bite every year, however, despite its reputation as the deadliest spider in the world, a study suggested that only just over two per cent of those bitten actually needed anti-venom – and this mainly applied to children – while other studies have shown that the venom is so toxic that it is exceptionally dangerous to humans. Some claims have been made in other studies that the Brazilian wandering spider actually only injects venom into one third of victims, however, with various subspecies of the spider living alongside it, unless the spider in question is formally identified there is no real way of knowing what the true figures are. However, the spider has proved that it is not afraid to attack should it feel threatened in any way.

lizards and mice. It is roughly four to five inches in length with exceptionally strong venom. It is quite likely without proper medical care and appropriate anti-venom that a bite from a Brazilian wandering spider will prove fatal. Often appearing quite nervous, the spider is highly agile and when it is disturbed assumes the position of standing on its hind limbs while keeping its front legs raised. It watches the movements of its

The Brazilian wandering spider is also related to the Brazilian Huntsman which is renowned for its venom – some class it as the most venomous spider in the world – and the Brazilian Armed spider which is extremely aggressive and has the largest venom glands of any spider. Sometimes confused with the tarantula, the Brazilian wandering spider is not even remotely related to the larger species. Hatchlings of the wandering spider eat tiny crickets and flightless fruit flies.

A chef from Somerset in the UK was bitten by a Brazilian wandering spider when it arrived hidden in a box of bananas at the pub where he worked. Despite the shock of being bitten by this venomous creature, he took a photo of the offending spider on his mobile phone. Experts at Bristol Zoo were able to identify the spider and suggest anti-venom. The chef was successfully treated at a local hospital where a member of staff – not realising that the spider was incredibly venomous – let the creature go in hospital grounds. In the ensuing panic, experts agreed that the spider would not have lived long after its release which gave some comfort to local residents.

Brown Recluse Spider

THE BROWN RECLUSE SPIDER belongs to a group of arachnids known as "recluse spiders" and is often referred to as the "violin" spider or "fiddleback" due to its violin-shaped markings on the cephalothorax. But there are times, such as when the spider has recently molted, that these markings are less distinct.

The brown recluse is native to North America while some non-native species have been found in isolated pockets of the US. Mainly found in the central midwestern states and down as far as the Gulf of Mexico, it is a venomous predator that should be regarded with caution. Its range follows a southerly direction from Nebraska through southern Iowa, Illinois and Indiana to southwest Ohio and in southern states it is native in central Texas to Georgia.

The abdomen of the brown recluse can vary in colour from dark brown to tan while the fine hairs that cover the spider give it a velvety look. It has long, thin legs which are also brown and can reach a fairly wide span. Males are typically slightly smaller than females although they have longer legs. This spider is unusual in that it has six eyes – as opposed to the usual eight – which are paired to the front of the head.

This spider is not particularly aggressive and will normally only bite if threatened, provoked or disturbed. However, these spiders are adept at hiding and if brushed against they will bite. Some unsuspecting victims have received a bite when putting on shoes in which a spider has been hiding. As with other spiders, some individuals are more sensitive to spider bites than others. But, reaction to a bite usually depends on the amount of venom injected. Many bites end with the victim only suffering a slight red mark and most will heal without severe scarring. Some bites are not noticed for several hours, while other people feel a small pinprick at the bite site.

Others are not so lucky and may experience a variety of symptoms which may include itching, vomiting, fever, muscle aches, joint pain and shock, while some may even experience even more acute problems such as a deep painful wound that takes a long time to heal. Severe reactions result in a deep wound that progressively gets bigger and bigger and can eventually reach the size of a hand span as tissue is slowly destroyed to reveal another layer of tissue beneath. This takes many weeks to heal and often leaves severe scarring. At worse, this type of reaction can eventually cause gangrene. Fatalities are very rare however the old, infirm and young children are most at risk and most likely to suffer from an extreme reaction to a bite. Treatments to curb problems can include elevating and immobilising the limb, the application of an ice pack to reduce swelling and aloe vera to soothe the pain. Prompt medical attention should be sought.

Due to regular misdiagnoses, there is now a test that can be carried out to determine whether the bite is from a brown recluse or not. This is important as misdiagnoses leads to incorrect treatments being administered.

Like the black widow and the Brazilian wandering spider, the brown recluse favours dark, quiet sites. It spins a tangled web which is where it spends its time during the day, although it is found hunting for food at night. This is also the time when mature males hunt in search of females. These spiders are at home either indoors or outdoors and can be found in basements, attics, folded sheets and clothes, wardrobes and behind furniture. They also like storage boxes. Outside they are found in barns, outbuildings and sheds as well as garages and other hiding places they can find in gardens.

A young brown recluse spider takes

about 12 months to mature into an adult and mature females typically lay their eggs between May and July. Up to 50 eggs are safely housed in a silken sac that is roughly two thirds of an inch in diameter. Spiderlings hatch in about four weeks and like other spiders find that their development is dependent on temperature, humidity and availability of food sources. However, the brown

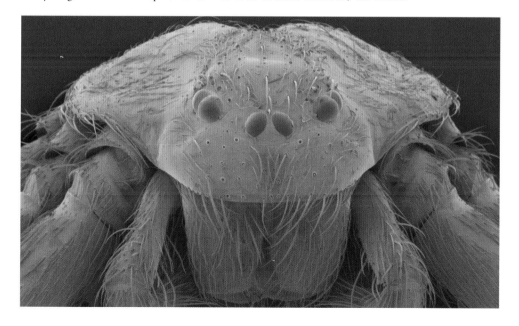

recluse can survive for up to six months without food or water and life expectancy is usually one or two years.

Funnel-web Spider

INCLUDING THREE TREE-DWELL-ing types, 36 species have been identified throughout eastern Australia and the state of Tasmania. Considered to be the third most dangerous spider in the world, the funnel-web can be found in coastal areas and forests where these arachnids like to burrow in cool, moist habitats. These include under rock crevices and rotting logs, while in gardens they favour rockeries and shrubs.

Funnel-webs like to keep themselves away from danger – including humans – but their burrows are easily spotted by the traces of irregular silk lines that are visible at the burrow entrance. Flooding of burrows does increase the spider's activity, but they are prone to drying out and need the security of moist conditions. They are largely nocturnal creatures. The Sydney funnel-web spider is found in New South Wales where it prefers the forest areas while those in more coastal regions require areas of sandy clay which retains moisture more readily.

A bite from a funnel-web is particularly dangerous for humans and can cause death. Summer – during December to February – is the most likely time to get bitten as this is when males are leaving their burrows in search of a mate. The male Sydney funnel-web is more dangerous than the female and this large spider injects highly toxic venom that attacks the nervous system. Female funnel-webs do not have this same capability. Bites cause pain, abdominal pain, vomiting, fever and numbness in the mouth. However, since the introduction of anti-venom no deaths have occurred. In the past, however, the Atrax genera of the funnel-web – only found in Sydney – killed 13 people, where seven of the victims were children.

The funnel-webs are known to bite successively and aggressively and can move quickly across ground. Death occurs due to progressive and severe hypotension and sometimes because of raised pressure in the brain as a result of cerebral oedema. It is always advisable to seek medical attention as soon as possible after a bite. Immediate first aid advice usually includes applying a pressure bandage, not a tourniquet, which will immobilise the affected area. If bitten on a limb, use a splint to further immobilise the wound area. Restrict movement and if at all possible, take the offending spider when seeking help so that a proper identification is given.

Cats and dogs as well as other mammals on the other hand seem relatively unaffected by funnel-web bites.

The spiders are fairly large in size with body lengths ranging from one centimetre to more than five centimetres. Their bodies are dark and colours of abdomens range from black to brown, while the front of the cephalothorax is glossy in appearance

with eyes grouped closely together. The funnel-web's large and powerful fangs point straight down and do not cross while their ample venom glands are rather small compared to a true tarantula – which is related to the funnel-web. So named, because of the funnel shaped web they weave in order to catch prey, funnel-webs mainly eat insects although they have been known to prey on lizards and frogs.

Female funnel-web spiders spend most of their life in a burrow while adult males leave their burrows to mate. Adult males sexually mature between two and four years and will only live for a further six to nine months after this time. As a result, they spend much of their adult life – in summer and autumn – searching for receptive females with which to mate. Males track down females in their hidden burrows by following the scent that a female gives off to signal that she is receptive. The male has to ensure that the female is restrained by the spurs on his second legs during mating otherwise she will strike him with her fangs. The silk egg sac – shaped like a pillow – contains in excess of 100 eggs which the female guards aggressively. Three weeks after

the eggs are laid, the spiderlings hatch and stay with their mother for a few months. They then leave to set up their own burrows. Young males will construct their own burrows where they will stay until they are sexually mature and have had their final adult molt. The life expectancy of female funnel-webs is much longer than that of males and they generally live for more than 10 years. Females only really venture from their burrows if they need to hunt at night.

Red Back Spider

THESE SMALL SPIDERS ARE RENowned for hiding under, and in, garden furniture, gazebos and sheds in gardens throughout Australia. Able to give a nasty bite, they present a significant risk to young children, the elderly and infirm, but it is unlikely that a red back will inject enough venom to seriously injure a fit adult.

Belonging to the Theridiidae family, the red back is closely related to the black widow spider of North America,

where the only visible distinction is a red stripe that follows the line of the abdomen in the Australian variety. The spider is also closely related to the European malmignatte, the jockey spider of Arabia and the black wolf in Russia. It is also related to the brown widow spider prevalent on the east coast of Australia.

Like other venomous spiders, the red back weaves a tangled web that looks messy and disorganised. However, the spider cleverly weaves an upper retreat that resembles a funnel in which to watch and wait. Red backs like habitats in close proximity to humans.

Perhaps it is this close proximity that results in the numerous red back bites that humans incur, particularly during the summer months. More than 275 requests are made for anti-venom each year. Only a bite from a female is dangerous and she is easily recognisable by her black abdomen with its dorsal red stripe and red spot on the underside. Young females have additional white markings on the abdomen. Females also typically have small round bodies of roughly 20-

40mm and long, thin shiny black legs. Male spiders are much smaller and are not easily detectable unless found near females. Males are also paler in colour and their fangs are not strong enough to penetrate human skin.

Bites can be fatal, but more often than not, cause uncomfortable symptoms such as pain, sweating, weakness in the muscles, nausea and vomiting. Since the introduction of anti-venom in 1956 there has only been one reported death, although red backs were responsible for a number of deaths until the mid-1950s. An ice pack applied to the bite site will alleviate pain – do not apply a pressure bandage as this pressure only worsens the pain of the slow moving venom and seek medical help as soon as possible.

Despite their fearsome reputation, red backs are not aggressive and if disturbed would rather run away than give you a nasty bite. They will only attack a human if their egg sacs are disturbed or there is nowhere to run to. Nets and mesh are advisable across doorways and windows to avoid the small arachnid entering a home and weaving a web, especially as they favour using window frames for this very purpose.

Red back spiders face the threat of other spiders that will prey on them, including the black house spider which is known to hunt and feed on the red back. If a homeowner finds that their house or garden is infested with venomous red backs then the black house spider is probably the best way to deal with the menace after a local pest control company. Although the black house spider can also bite, this species is not nearly as dangerous to man.

The origins of the red back are not well documented, but it is thought that human activities throughout the 19th century contributed to its distribution throughout Australia. In more recent times, red backs have become fairly prevalent in Japan. There are also small colonies in New Zealand where the red backs hitched a lift on the poles shipped from Australia for electric power and telephone cables.

Red back spiders feed on a variety of small insects and other, smaller species of spider. Once prey has been caught in its web, the red back races down to wrap the victim in a band of silk. The spider then bites the prey and takes it to its funnel retreat where it sucks on the prey until it is dry. The skeleton of the prey is then conveniently left outside the web.

Red backs rest in their web during the day which is usually hidden and they will hang upside down outside the web during the evening.

Tarantula

TARANTULAS ARE FOUND WORLD-wide and across North America to the southern and southwest states. Related to the desert tarantula, this species is relatively small and usually only has a body length of less than two inches. Its cousin, found in the deserts of Arizona, New Mexico and Southern California is generally an inch bigger. Other tarantulas are prevalent in South America including Mexico, Asia, the south of Europe, Africa and Australia.

The tarantula is also closely related to the funnel-web spider, although is not the deadly spider that its Australian relative is renowned for being. The Eurypelma californicum is the most common type of tarantula found in North America that spins large webs and eats small birds. The majority of the many species of tarantula are coloured black or brown. Others, however, have distinctive markings including the Cobalt Blue tarantula which has deep blue legs while the Mexican red-legged tarantula has bright red markings. The Goliath tarantula is one of the larger species and has a body length that can reach up to five inches while its leg span is around 12 inches.

With its customary eight eyes which sit closely together, the tarantula is capable of producing a hissing sound by rubbing its jaws together. These large arachnids have two large fangs but are

rather slow when manoeuvring and spend the majority of their time hiding in burrows. They are active from spring to autumn during the late afternoon. As well as the usual hairs covering their bodies, some have a dense covering of hairs called urticating hairs which are used as protection against enemies. These fine hairs are barbed and do contain some venom. Some tarantulas with these hairs can even launch them at a predator about to attack it, however, they also use them for marking territory or to line their burrows.

The chances of being bitten by a tarantula are rare, and despite its worrying appearance, a bite from this spider won't actually kill a human. The venom causes slight swelling to the bite site and is often accompanied by some numbness and itching which is short-lived. However, the bite itself is relatively painful. Tarantulas are not aggressive by nature and will not attack a human unless threatened or provoked. A tarantula bite is one of the rare instances where it is acceptable to clean the site of the wound with soap and water which protects against infection.

Tarantulas prefer to live in dry habitats and often choose the abandoned homes of other creatures in which to make their burrows rather than building their own. Nocturnal by nature, tarantulas catch prey by moving at speed and typically eat insects like grasshoppers and beetles, smaller spiders and occasionally lizards. Tarantulas attack their prey with their fangs injecting venom while grasping the prey so it cannot escape. The spider grinds its victim and secretes digestive juices all over it before sucking up the juices from the prey.

These spiders reach sexual maturity after several years. A mature male is usually black whereas the female tends to be brown. During the autumn females leave a scent signalling to the male that she is receptive for mating. Mating takes place after a courtship "dance" and males typically die a few months after mating, unless the female has eaten him before mating has had a chance to take place. However, females have a life expectancy of 25 years or more during which time they regularly produce eggs.

The female stores the male's sperm in receptacles and immediately before fertilisation lays the eggs with a mixture of sperm. These are laid in a cocoon which the female has constructed in her burrow. As soon as all the eggs are released the female closes up the cocoon. The young hatch around six to nine weeks later and after a further two or three weeks are then ready to leave their mother and find burrows of their own.

Tarantulas often find themselves the prey of other predators including snakes, lizards and spider-eating birds including the Tarantula hawk. However, it is the large wasp that is its worst enemy and once the spider is paralysed by the wasp's deadly sting, the wasp then drags the tarantula to its own burrow where it lays its eggs in the spider's abdomen before sealing it in the burrow. The wasp larvae then feed from the tarantula.

ALSO AVAILABLE IN THIS SERIES

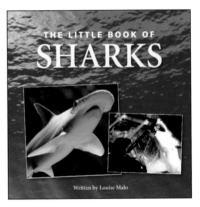

The pictures in this book were provided courtesy of the following:

GETTY IMAGES
101 Bayham Street, London NW1 0AG

SHUTTERSTOCK IMAGES
www.shutterstock.com

Design and artwork by David Wildish

Creative Director Kevin Gardner

Published by Green Umbrella Publishing

Publishers Jules Gammond and Vanessa Gardner

Written by Louise Malo